STOP CODEPENDENCY

Learn How to End Once and for All
Codependent Relationships and Love Yourself

Henry Baldwin

STOP CODEPENDENCY

CONTENTS

STOP CODEPENDENCY

INTRODUCTION

Codependency is often referred to as the addiction of love. The negative effects of codependency are far-reaching and typically occur within a mismatched emotional relationship. Codependency is essential, a coping mechanism used to lessen emotional pain. It is a compulsive behavior that has been absorbed throughout life in order to avoid pain which may be perceived but perhaps not really. If you are concerned about your own relationship currently, consider whether it is consistently an uphill struggle as you try to resolve issues. Evaluate whether your relationship is forged on a basis of emotional conflict and whether you are constantly trying to resolve your partner's problems for them by facing these burdens willingly. If yes, then this is fairly typical of codependent relationships.

Codependency quite simply is a relationship addiction and can affect all types of relationships from family, to friends, to romantic relationships. Within your partnership, you may feel that you are helping to overcome issues by being the strong assertive one, but in reality, you may be hindering your relationship with your partner. It may feel as if your own behavior is normal and that you are simply trying to help your partner to rebuild his or her life, but you need to establish whether you are simply being helpful or whether it is a pre-learned need within you to continuously help, to assume control and yet to put the needs of others first. Doing this with complete honesty will help you determine whether you or not you truly have a love addiction.

The Definition of Codependency
Codependency is defined as a dysfunctional relationship in which a person is more concerned about the needs of others than his or her own needs. It is often characterized by

excessive care-taking, enabling, controlling, and/or an unhealthy need for recognition or approval.

Codependency is a learned behavior that can be passed down from one generation to another. It is an emotional and behavioral condition that affects an individual's ability to have a healthy, mutually satisfying relationship. It is also known as "relationship addiction" because people with codependency often form or maintain relationships that are one-sided, emotionally destructive and/or abusive.

Characteristics of codependent People are:
1.   Low self-esteem often projected onto others.
2.   Being either super responsible or super irresponsible.
3.   A tendency to confuse love and pity, with the tendency to "love" people they can pity and rescue
4.   Lack of self-confidence in making decisions, no sense of power in making choices.
5.   A tendency to do more than their share, all of the time
6.   Feeling of fear, insecurity, inaequacy, guilt, hurt, and shame which are denied.
7.   The tendency to become hurt when people don't recognize their efforts
8.   Isolation and fear of people, resentment of authority figures.
9.   An unhealthy dependence on relationships. The co-dependent will do anything to hold on to a relationship; to avoid the feeling of abandonment
10.   Fear of anger or bottling anger up till it explodes.
11.   An extreme need for approval and recognition
12.   Hypersensitivity to criticism.
13.   Being addicted to excitement/drama.
14.   A sense of guilt when asserting themselves
15.   A compelling need to control others
16.   The tendency to look for "victims" to help.
17.   Rigidity and need to control.

18. Lack of trust in self and/or others
19. Lies, when it would be just as easy, to tell the truth.
20. Fear of being abandoned or alone
21. Difficulty identifying feelings
22. Overreacting to change.
23. Constantly seeking approval and affirmation, yet having a compromised sense of self.
24. Problems with intimacy/boundaries
25. Chronic anger
26. Poor communications
27. Inability to see alternatives to situations, thus responding very impulsively.
28. Feelings of being different.

Who Does Co-dependency Affect?

Co-dependency often affects a spouse, a parent, sibling, friend, or co-worker of a person afflicted with alcohol or drug dependence. Originally, co-dependent was a term used to describe partners in chemical dependency, persons living with, or in a relationship with an addicted person. Similar patterns have been seen in people in relationships with chronically or mentally ill individuals. Today, however, the term has broadened to describe any co-dependent person from any dysfunctional family.

How Do Co-dependent People Behave?

Co-dependents have low self-esteem and look for anything outside of themselves to make them feel better. They find it hard to "be themselves." Some try to feel better through alcohol, drugs or nicotine - and become addicted. Others may develop compulsive behaviors like workaholism, gambling, or indiscriminate sexual activity.

They have good intentions. They try to take care of a person who is experiencing difficulty, but the caretaking becomes compulsive and defeating. Co-dependents often take on a martyr's role and become "benefactors" to an individual in need. A wife may cover for her alcoholic husband; a mother may make excuses for a truant child, or a father may "pull some strings" to keep his child from suffering the consequences of delinquent behavior.

The problem is that these repeated rescue attempts allow the needy individual to continue on a destructive course and to become even more dependent on the unhealthy caretaking of the "benefactor." As this reliance increases, the co-dependent develops a sense of reward and satisfaction from "being needed." When the caretaking becomes compulsive, the co-dependent feels choiceless and helpless in the relationship but is unable to break away from the cycle of behavior that causes it. Co-dependents view themselves as victims and are attracted to that same weakness in love and friendship relationships.

If you feel that you might be in a codependent relationship, consider whether deep down, your self-esteem and sense of self-worth might be low as this is fairly typical, although often these negative feelings are kept hidden and a stronger persona presented to the world. If you cast your mind back to your own previous relationships, you may be able to detect any familiar patterns where you have assumed the strong, caring role in each of them. The external influences within each relationship may be very different but the cause can be deeply rooted and parallel.

To identify whether you are codependent, ask yourself the following questions:

- Do you spend a great deal of time and energy on caring for your partners' needs?
- Do you sacrifice your own needs to enable them to achieve theirs?
- Do you find it difficult to say no?
- If you were unable to help your partner, would you experience feelings of guilt and unworthiness?
- Do you sometimes feel that you are a caregiver as opposed to a partner?
- Do you tend to control situations with other people

because it makes you feel safer?

- Do you feel guilty for someone else when they act inappropriately in public, and perhaps even try to cover it up for them?

- Is it hard for you to say "no" when someone else asks you for help, even if helping would be inconvenient for you?

- Do you remain loyal to people who are harmful to you?

- Do you place a high value on someone else's approval of your behavior or feelings?

The more you identify with the words above, the further to the right you fall on the Human Interdependence Spectrum (and the more likely you are to be codependent).

If you feel that any or all of these questions are relative to you then it is worth acknowledging that you may need to speak to a professional counselor for help. If you start to feel introverted, confused and guilty, then stop and acknowledge that it is not your fault if you have become involved within a cycle of toxic relationships. Realization is vital and it will afford you greater clarity going forward. Just remember that codependent relationships are not uncommon and you need to establish why you are drawn to certain people if you have any chance of leaving this addiction of love behind.

A codependency addiction may not be easy to cure, but the speed of recovery is very much on an individual basis and this is something that a counselor can discuss with you. Facing up to the reality is paramount and recognizing that you are not to blame will also help to start the healing process, but the most important part of turning your life around is having the will to do so. The healing process will truly begin once you become aware of the full reasoning behind your love addiction. Once the negative aspects of codependent relationships can be controlled, new healthier patterns can be formed so that future relationships are based on equal emotional stability and input.

The Truth About Codependency

Codependency is just an unhealthy relational style. It's a condition that is developed, usually as a cause of upsetting childhood ordeals. It's not a mental disease or "something that you're created with." And it can be altered.

Where It Comes From

If you grew up in a place where your psychological and mental or physical needs were not attained, you possibly came up with the rationale, "If I'm adequate, then someone will at some point care about me."

Among the most appropriate ways to "be adequate" was to begin caring for other people, most importantly the older people in your life that had significant emotional needs.

Sometimes those adults were addicts. Maybe, these people were emotionally, physically, or even sexually abusive. While that relational style made sense earlier, that same relational style is starting to backfire at this time. Instead of gaining the love you hope and require, it's beginning to become uncontrollable.

That's purely because your meaning of looking after others includes controlling their thoughts, feelings, and emotions. It will require you to drop your own needs and is causing you to become resentful and dejected most of the time.

You've never developed how to be liable for yourself, and, more importantly, never learned how to enable some people to be responsible for their own decisions and feelings.

The minute you know how to do that, you will refrain from being codependent and embark on living inter-dependently with people.

Roots of Codependency

Codependency commonly has its roots in dysfunctional families. A child who is not properly taken care of begins to think his needs are not important and can be ignored. The child is brought up among cold and uncaring members in the dysfunctional family. As a result, even as an adult the victim gets attracted to emotionally uncaring people, the very type that needs to avoid. This leads to the development of unhealthy and damaging relationships which cause much suffering and pain to the codependent.

Child in a Dysfunctional Family

A child raised in a dysfunctional family suffers negative emotions such as shame, pain, anger, fear, etc that are denied or ignored as the family does not acknowledge these problems. As a result, the child learns to repress its emotions and ignore its needs and feelings, leading to a lack of self-confidence and self-esteem. The child does not get any physical affection and there is no trust or honesty among the family members. To compound the issue, the child thinks this dysfunctional lifestyle is normal. Hence it grows up to be an emotionally immature adult resulting in codependent behavior.

Additional Descriptions of Codependency

Codependency is the altered belief system wherein you truly feel that you are definitely not as good as all others.

Others have worth, but you don't.

Due to the fact of that contorted belief system, you're always placing other people's wishes before your own and tend to ignore or discount your own personal feelings.

Your sense of self-esteem has becomes exclusively dependent upon your capability to satisfy everyone around you. If you're in a position to look after everyone's needs regardless of the cost to you, then you can consider yourself a good person.

Some people call codependency a "relationship addiction."

It is the irresistible impulse to always be thinking about someone else, even though you don't want to.

It's definitely not selflessness. Selflessness is a choice. Selflessness comes out of an overflow of your love and worth for yourself.

With codependency, you're held hostage by your own sense of guilt and shame if you don't give support to other people.

You have faith that you might be better able to look after someone than they are themselves.

What Codependency is Not

Now, let's dispel some myths and set realistic expectations before we go any deeper.

1.   Codependency does NOT mean you're just really nice and helpful. Nowadays people tend to throw the word around like a frisbee, but real codependency does not simply mean you're extremely kindhearted and willing to do things for other people. It means crossing the line between healthy interdependence and help that hurts. A codependent's "help" usually involves anxiety, discomfort, and feeling out of control, because the motivation behind the help isn't just for the sake of helping, it's done in order to avoid a catastrophe of some sort.

2.   Codependents do NOT always come from families with alcoholics. Even though the word was coined for the family members of alcoholics as part of Alcoholics Anonymous, the effects of codependency seems to originate from a variety of causes, often involving some sort of trauma, pronounced or subtle. People who grow up in "normal" environments may still have circumstances that create feelings of shame, unresolved grief or abandonment, all of which can cause codependent tendencies. So, codependency is often thought of on a sliding scale, and anyone can suffer from it.

3.   Codependency is NOT just for women. While

there's an 85% chance that you're female, both women and men can have codependency issues.

1.2 Symptoms of Codependency

The term codependency has been around for almost four decades. Although it originally applied to spouses of alcoholics, first called co-alcoholics, research revealed that the characteristics of codependents were much more prevalent in the general population than had been imagined. In fact, they found that if you were raised in a dysfunctional family or had an ill parent, it's likely that you're codependent. Don't feel bad if that includes you. Most families in America are dysfunctional, so that covers just about everyone, you're in the majority! They also found that codependent symptoms got worse if untreated, but the good news was that they were reversible.

Here's a list of symptoms. You don't need to have all of them to qualify as codependent.

1.   Low self-esteem
Not feeling that you're good enough or comparing yourself to others is a sign of low self-esteem. The tricky thing about self-esteem is that some people think highly of themselves, but it's only a camouflage for really feeling unlovable or inadequate. Underneath, usually hidden from consciousness, are feelings of shame. Some of the things that go along with low self-esteem are guilt feelings and perfectionism. If everything is perfect, you don't feel bad about yourself.

2.   People pleasing

It's fine to want to please someone you care about, but codependents usually don't think they have a choice. Saying "No" causes them anxiety. Some codependents have a hard time saying "No" to anyone. They go out of their way and sacrifice their own needs to accommodate other people.

3.   Poor Boundaries

Boundaries are sort of an imaginary line between you and others. It divides up what's yours and somebody else's, and that applies not only to your body, money, and belongings but also to your feelings, thoughts, and needs. That's especially where codependents get into trouble. They have blurry or weak boundaries between themselves and others. They feel responsible for other people's feelings and problems or blame their own on someone else.

Some codependents have rigid boundaries. They are closed off and withdrawn, making it hard for other people to get close to them. Sometimes, people flip back and forth between having weak boundaries and rigid ones.

4.   Reactivity

A consequence of poor boundaries is that you react to everyone's thoughts and feelings. If someone says something you disagree with, you either believe it or become defensive. You absorb their words because there's no boundary. With a boundary, you'd realize it was just their opinion and not a reflection of you and not feel threatened by disagreements.

5.   Caretaking

Another effect of poor boundaries is that if someone else has a problem, you want to help them to the point that you give up yourself. It's natural to feel empathy and sympathy for someone, but codependents start putting other people ahead of themselves. In fact, they need to help and might feel rejected if another person doesn't want help. Moreover, they keep trying to help and fix the other person, even when that person clearly isn't taking their advice.

6.   Control

Control helps codependents feel safe and secure. Everyone needs some control over events in their life. You wouldn't want to live in constant uncertainty and chaos, but for codependents, control limits their ability to take risks and share their feelings. Sometimes they have an addiction that either helps them loosen up, like alcoholism, or helps them hold their feelings down, like workaholism so that they don't feel out of control.

Codependents also need to control those close to them, because they need other people to behave in a certain way to feel okay. In fact, people pleasing and caretaking can be used to control and manipulate people. Alternatively, codependents are bossy and tell you what you should or shouldn't do. This is a violation of someone else's boundary.

7.   Dysfunctional communication

Codependents have trouble when it comes to communicating their thoughts, feelings, and needs. Of course, if you don't know what you think, feel or need, this becomes a problem. Other times, you know, but you won't own up to your truth. You're afraid to be truthful because you don't want to upset someone else. Instead of saying, "I don't like that," you might pretend that it's okay or tell someone what to do. Communication becomes dishonest and confusing when you try to manipulate the other person out of fear.

8.   Obsessions

Codependents have a tendency to spend their time thinking about other people or relationships. This is caused by their dependency and anxieties and fears. They can also become obsessed when they think they've made or might make a "mistake."

Sometimes you can lapse into fantasy about how you'd like things to be or about someone you love as a way to avoid the pain of the present. This is one way to stay in denial, discussed below, but it keeps you from living your life.

9. Dependency

Codependents need other people to like them to feel okay about themselves and they're afraid of being rejected or abandoned - even if they can function on their own. Others need to always be in a relationship because they feel depressed or lonely when they're by themselves for too long. This trait makes it hard for them to end a relationship, even when the relationship is painful or abusive. They end up feeling trapped.

10. Denial

One of the problems people face in getting help for codependency is that they're in denial about it, meaning that they don't face their problem. Usually, they think the problem is someone else or the situation. They either keep complaining or trying to fix the other person, or go from one relationship or job to another and never own up the fact that they have a problem.

Codependents also deny their feelings and needs. Often times, they don't know what they're feeling and are instead focused on what others are feeling. The same thing goes for their needs. They pay attention to other people's needs and not their own. They might be in denial of their need for space and autonomy. Although some codependents seem needy, others act like they're self-sufficient when it comes to needing help. They won't reach out and have trouble receiving. They are in denial of their vulnerability and need for love and intimacy.

11. Problems with intimacy

This not referring to sex, although sexual dysfunction is

often a reflection of an intimacy problem. It is being open and close with someone in an intimate relationship. Because of the shame and weak boundaries, you might fear that you'll be judged, rejected, or left. On the other hand, you may fear smothered in a relationship and losing your autonomy. You might deny your need for closeness and feel that your partner wants too much of your time; your partner complains that you're unavailable, but he or she is denying his or her need for separateness.

12. Painful emotions

Codependency creates stress and leads to painful emotions. Shame and low self-esteem create anxiety and fear about:

- Being Judged
- Being rejected or abandoned
- Making mistakes
- Being a failure
- Being close and feeling trapped
- Being alone

The other symptoms lead to feelings of anger and resentment, depression, hopelessness, and despair. When the feelings are too much, you can feel numb.

There is help for recovery and change. The first step is getting guidance and support. These symptoms are deeply ingrained habits and difficult to identify and change on your own. Join a Twelve Step program, such as Codependents Anonymous or seek counseling. Work on becoming more assertive and building your self-esteem.

Other Signs Of Codependency Includes

1. Feeling responsible for solving others' problems. The codependent feels the need to solve another's problems. The codependent believes that their help is needed. They feel that the person in need cannot manage to make the right decisions or take the right actions to solve his or her own

problem.

2.   Offering advice to others whether it is asked for or not. The codependent jumps at the opportunity to provide "much-needed" advice. The codependent offers an endless stream of good advice regardless of whether the advice has been asked for or not.

3.   Expecting others to do what the codependent says. Once advice has been given, the codependent expects the advice to be followed. Codependents often do not understand boundaries.

4.   The codependent feels used and underappreciated. The codependent will expend enormous amounts of energy to take charge of another's life. This is all under the guise of sincerely wanting to help. When the help or advice is ignored or rejected, the codependent feels angry, abused, and unappreciated.

5.   Trying to please people so others will like or love the codependent. Codependents will go out of their way to please another person. They hope to receive love, approval or be accepted and liked. If the approval is not given, the codependent will feel victimized.

6.   Taking everything personally. Because there are little to no boundaries, any remark, comment or action is a reflection back upon the codependent. This makes the need to feel in control paramount.

7.   Feeling like a victim. Everything that happens either to the codependent or the loved one is a reflection on the codependent. Such people usually feel victimized and powerless and do not understand their role in creating their own reality.

8.   Using manipulation, shame, or guilt to control others' behavior. To get their way codependents will respond in a fashion that will force compliance by others. These tactics may be unconscious. Since everyone else's behavior is a reflection on the codependent, it is important that the codependent feel in control.

9.   Lying to themselves and making excuses for others'

bad behavior. Because codependents do not deal directly with their feelings, they develop techniques to lie to themselves about others' behaviors. Because they feel responsible for others' behaviors, they will rationalize and blame others for their loved one's poor behavior or blame themselves for another's poor behavior, seeking to maintain control.

10. Fearing rejection and being unlovable. The codependent fears that if he or she is not successful at everything, or indeed expresses his/her feelings or needs, they will be rejected. In a codependent's way of thinking, he or she will be unlovable. A codependent does not trust others easily or share openly because he or she will be exposed.

Questions to Ask About Codependent Behavior
1.   Do you avoid confrontation?
2.   Do you neglect your needs to attend to another's first?
3.   Do you accept verbal or physical abuse by others?
4.   Do take responsibility for the actions of others?
5.   Do you feel shame when others make mistakes?
6.   Do you do more than your share at work, at home or in organizations?
7.   Do you ask for help?
8.   Do you need others' validation to feel good about yourself?
9.   Do you think everyone's feelings are more important than your own?
10. Do you suffer from low self-esteem?

Many times, codependents will turn to addictive behaviors themselves to negotiate their unresolved feelings. They will use substances such as alcohol, drugs, or food to stuff their emotions. Or, they will engage in risky behaviors. When a codependent gets tangled in the web of drug addiction or alcoholism, he or she can quickly lose control.

Not only will the addict's disease progress, but the codependent's disorder will worsen. Mental and physical well-being becomes impossible. Drug and alcohol rehab will address these issues and teach you what to look for in codependent behavior.

5 Steps on How to Break Codependency Habits
Now that you understand the impact of codependency, you may be more motivated to undergo the often-difficult task of overcoming it.

Below are five steps to help you on your journey:
1.   Learn to love yourself
This is the catch-all solution for avoiding and overcoming codependency. People who love and respect themselves have boundaries for the types of people they'll stay in relationships with. They won't crave affection from just anyone. They're able to leave a partner who isn't right for them and therefore won't fall in codependency. However, if you suffered from a difficult upbringing, learning to love yourself may not be easy.

Below, are some practical steps to help you engage in self-love.
Write a self-love list: complete a list of 50 things you love about yourself. Include past achievements, physical attributes, likable parts of your personality and anything else you can think of. Feel free to add weaknesses that you're attempting to improve upon, too. The fact you're bothering to better yourself at all makes this list-worthy.
Fifty is A LOT. The challenge is supposed to be difficult, so it forces you to dig deep and uncover everything you appreciate about yourself.
The result is a huge helping of self-love. Those who believe in the power of affirmations may want to read their list every day. Either way, the fact that you managed to write 50 items should provide a jolt of self-esteem during difficult moments.

2. Start a gratitude journal

If you start a gratitude journal, you'll be joining worldwide names such as Tony Robbins, Arianna Huffington, and Oprah Winfrey in doing so.

There are many forms of gratitude journals, but many people use it to list five things they're grateful for each morning and five achievements they're proud of every evening. Nothing is too insignificant to be listed.

3. Meditation

Meditation is the practice of staying in the present moment, rather than listening to your internal voices.

It's fantastic for improving focus, calming anxiety, and reducing stress. If your inner voices constantly remind you of your fears and insecurities, it could be a great habit for increasing your self-love too.

In fact, it's possible to focus your meditation on gratitude and self-love.

4. Develop hobbies and passions

If you find an activity you're truly passionate about, this will go a long way in stopping you from worrying about your relationship status. The best hobbies for overcoming codependency are those you can engage in alone. Your passion should allow you to garner a flow state that makes the hours fly by without you even noticing. Many athletes describe experiencing this sensation during sports. Musicians experience the same while practicing their instruments as do artists in the middle of their latest creation.

Your passion doesn't have to involve talent. It can be as simple as reading or listening to music, provided that it makes you satisfied in your own company. If you haven't found a passion, that's a fantastic excuse to try new activities. Meetup.com is a brilliant website, which will list plenty of ideas in your local area.

Of course, you can engage in hobbies with your friends, too. Just don't become too dependent on their company for a good time.

5.   Gain romantic abundance

Most people fall into codependence because they feel their destructive relationship is their only chance for love. They cling to that unhealthy person because they believe no one else will have them.

As such, a great step for overcoming codependency is to gain romantic abundance. This might be a more long-winded step than the others, but it remains important. If you're not currently abundant with romantic options, you may have to indulge in self-improvement and that's absolutely fine.

Learning to love yourself will do loads to gain you more romantic options. Indulging in hobbies, nurturing friendships, and leading a life that other people want to be a part of will also help. Making an effort to meet more people, whether that's through social events or dating apps like Tinder is another great idea.

You can work on your appearance, perhaps by exercising or updating your fashion. But it's the added confidence from the other steps listed above that'll do the most to attract more love interests into your life. This work will make you less attached to lovers who are wrong for you and give you the ability to choose your best fit from a bigger field of people.

Tips For Recognizing Codependency Symptoms

Codependency symptoms can be easy to identify when you know what to look for. One of the cornerstones of a healthy relationship is an equal emotional contribution from both partners. An imbalance at this level can cause a variety of problems and lead to codependency. It is characterized by constant internal and external conflict and struggles to satisfy the wants and needs of a partner in a relationship. One person tends to invest and sacrifice much more than the other, which can damage psychological health and self-esteem. Codependency erodes relationships and can threaten your well-being.

If you suspect you or your partner may be codependent, ask yourself the following questions:

• Do I have a history of insecurities in my relationships?
• Do I feel like I need to be in control all the time to make everyone happy?
• Do I avoid confrontations, even over things I think are important?
• Do I have unintentional feelings, like jealousy or an urgent need to have sex?
• Do I feel trapped or stuck in my relationships?
• Are there a large number of things I don't feel comfortable doing or talking about with my partner?

If you answered yes to several of these questions, there's a possibility you're participating in a codependent relationship.

A common theme among codependents is a childhood of rough and unloving relationships. This can include abuse by parents, rejection by early romantic interests, or the death of a close family member or friend. This can subconsciously drive codependents to put a disproportionate amount of effort into relationships in an effort to gain approval and love. The drive caused by this childhood vacuum can create codependency symptoms the mind uses to compensate. Since young people are so impressionable, they find these actions to be fulfilling, at least in the short-term. The mind searches for defense mechanisms and eagerly grabs anything that eases the pain of abuse, rejection, or loss. At this age, habits form quickly and can eventually become full-blown codependency.

Although codependency symptoms may seem harmless, they are actually very destructive. Though these thoughts and actions may ease the pain temporarily, they're no more than a band-aid for a larger wound. If you're worried you might have codependency symptoms, you're doing no one a favor by ignoring or tolerating them. If you value your relationships and, more importantly, yourself, then you are encouraged to take steps toward recovery.

It's not easy to shake any type of habit. However; the longer you wait, the more difficult it will be. Like most psychological issues, codependency can be cured over time with a strong will and external support. If you're unable or unsure how to break the cycle yourself, you can seek assistance from specialists who will help identify the causes of your love addiction and guide you to recovery. If you feel you are suffering from codependency symptoms, it's important to remember that you're not alone. Although almost all relationships exhibit a certain degree of codependency, it's the extreme cases that need corrective action. Take responsibility and confront your problem. It may be painful to deal with these issues, but it's the best way to love and value yourself and your relationship.

1.3   Types of Codependency

Learn Your Brand of Codependency and Triggers

It's true. Once used as a blanket term for family members of alcoholics, (codependency) as we know it nowadays entails up to four unique but sometimes related behavior patterns. They are:

1.   Self-Sacrifice: This is the classic behavior pattern most closely resembling the original label for codependents. Self-Sacrificers are rescuers and fixers. They are strong, proactive, the quintessential "battle axe". They often see others' needs as greater than their own, care-take, and give unsolicited advice. They feel inadequate, guilty, and selfish when they see someone in need and don't help.

2.   Subjugation: These are the people-pleasers who do it out of fear of retaliation and judgment. They don't express their thoughts or feelings easily and don't want to be rejected. They avoid confrontation at all costs and almost always capitulate when someone is angry with them, or they're asked to do something.

3.   Approval Seeking: Their primary motivation is to be liked, applauded, recognized and congratulated. Approval seekers often go along with popular opinion in order to avoid conflict and keep the peace. They're frequently asking themselves, "Did I do a good job?" "Does that person like me?" "Will this person or group approve of my words and actions?"

4.   Unrelenting Standards: The Perfectionists. These people judge themselves (and others) against high standards, and can come across as controlling or stressed. They're driven by fear of failure, inadequacy, and criticism. They're often workaholics, judgmental, and tend to have a strong case of the "the shoulds". (I should have done this better. You should have said that differently.)

Reading this list probably helped you identify strongly with at least one of these descriptions. This is important because identifying your brand of codependency makes it easier to identify your personal triggers so you can overcome them.

CHAPTER 2

WHAT IS CODEPENDENT RELATIONSHIP?

Codependent relationship as a specific type of dysfunctional helping relationship. Broadly speaking, in dysfunctional helping relationships, one person's help supports (enables) the other's underachievement, irresponsibility, immaturity, addiction, procrastination, or poor mental or physical health.

The helper does this by doing such things as rescuing the other from self-imposed predicaments, bearing their negative consequences for them, accommodating their unhealthy or irresponsible behaviors, and taking care of them such that they don't develop or exhibit competencies normal for those of their age or abilities. Although these unbalanced relationships can go on for some time, they are ultimately unsustainable due to their consumption of the helper's physical, emotional, or financial resources, and because they lead to resentment and relationship strain.

Dysfunctional helping relationships don't necessarily involve codependence, but they may. Codependent relationships are close relationships where much of the love

27

and intimacy in the relationship is experienced in the context of one person's distress and the other's rescuing or enabling. The helper shows love primarily through the provision of assistance and the other feels loved primarily when they receive assistance. The intense shared experiences of the other's struggles and disasters and the helper's rescues deepen the emotional connection and feelings of intimacy.

In the codependent relationship, the helper's emotional enmeshment leads them to keenly feel the other's struggles and to feel guilt at the thought of limiting their help or terminating the relationship. This motivates them to reduce the other's suffering (and their own) by continued helping and makes them quick to back off of any limits they set.

Helpers prone to codependent relationships often find intimacy in relationships where their primary role is that of rescuer, supporter, and confidante. These helpers are often dependent on the other's poor functioning to satisfy emotional needs such as the need to feel needed, and the need to keep the other close due to fears of abandonment. Feeling competent (relative to the other) also boosts the low self-esteem of some helpers.

In the codependent relationship, the other's dependence on the helper is also profound. The other is bound to the helper because the helper's lengthy aid has impeded their maturity, life skills, or confidence, or enabled their addiction, or poor mental or physical health, making them dependent on the helper's assistance. Their poor functioning brings them needed love, care, and concern from the helper, further reducing their motivation to change.

Due to their below average functioning, these others may have few relationships as close as their relationship with the helper. This makes them highly dependent on the helper to satisfy many of the needs met by close relationships (such as the need to matter to someone and the need for care). It is this high degree of a mutual, unhealthy dependence on the part of both the helper and the other that makes the relationship "codependent" and resistant to change.

While it's true that some dysfunctional helping relationships are indeed codependent, and it's also true that codependence may arise from some of your personality traits, be cautious in your adoption of the co-dependent moniker. Or at least don't wave it around like a flag of fate ("I'm codependent and I can't help myself because that's just what I do!"). And keep in mind that dysfunctional helping is complex. It's motivated by a variety of factors and shouldn't be reduced to simple notions of codependence.

Codependency is both a behavioral and emotional condition in which a person in a relationship feels that their happiness and self-worth depends upon another person. Codependents tend to form what can be called "relationship addiction", even though the relationship may actually have many problems. Many times one partner in the codependent relationship has a drug or alcohol addiction, but that is not always the case. The codependent may focus all of their efforts on the other person while putting their own needs aside. Codependency can occur with all types of relationships, not just marriages or romantic partnerships. It is possible to have codependency in friendships, family, community, or work relationships as well.

Low Self Esteem

Many codependents suffer from feelings of low self-esteem, which only fosters this type of dysfunctional relationship. They may feel that they need to stay put in their relationship even though it is not truly making them happy or meeting their emotional needs because they feel that no one else would want them. Because of their negative feelings about themselves due to the low self-esteem, the codependent may find themselves finding some type of comfort in their current relationship even when it is not a healthy one. The self-esteem issues can make codependents convince themselves that they need to stay in the relationship and put up with a less than desirable situation because they feel they are no good. For example, with an abusive alcoholic and a codependent, the person with low self-esteem may feel it is their duty to stay and cater to the needs of the person with the addiction and try to" fix" them and their relationship when in reality they should walk away.

Difficulty Setting Boundaries

People with codependency issues have difficulty setting boundaries in a relationship. They may allow others to invade their personal space and may feel as if they do not have the right to refuse to go along with what the other person is doing or thinking. They might feel as if they cannot disagree or have their own thoughts and opinions about anything, especially if it goes against what the other person in the relationship believes, feels, or thinks. The codependent may not even realize that they have the right to be treated with respect. In a healthy relationship, a person will establish these boundaries as a natural way to protect themselves while still having healthy and happy relationships with others.

Difficulty Owning Own Thoughts and Feelings

The codependent also has difficulty in owning their own thoughts and feelings, because they are so continually focused on the thoughts and needs of someone else. They spend their life trying so hard to please the other person and feed off of the approval and admiration of others. Somehow in all of this, their own true sense of self gets lost to the point where the codependent may not even really understand what he or she is really thinking or feeling because they so seldom focus on themselves.

Difficulty Meeting Own Wants and Needs

Those suffering from codependency have difficulty meeting their own wants and needs because of their reliance on the other person in the relationship. In cases of codependency, the codependent abandons their own self and is not even in tune to their own wants and needs. Always placing the other person before themselves becomes a way of life, and their own wants and needs are placed on the back burner.

Codependent Relationships: What's In It For Me?

The short answer to this question is nothing unless you want to be treated disrespectfully, constantly let down, or even abused. There is a fine line between a healthy devotion to a relationship and a destructive obsession over control and emotional validation. Codependency is a psychological state your mind develops to rationalize and minimize emotional pain. It often comes as a result of an uneven relationship, where the participants have different expectations and levels of commitment. Codependent relationships can become a lifelong habit with family, friends, and romantic interests if the symptoms go unchecked.

Characteristics of this love addiction include constant, repeated struggle and attempts to gain emotional control over the other member of the relationship. Resolution is an uphill struggle, and the codependent member will go to great lengths to please his or her partner. If these characteristics describe your relationship, then it's possible that you're in a codependent relationship. Typically, you go to great extremes on a repeated basis to control and regulate your partner's emotions. By being assertive, you attempt to keep others content and keep things from getting out of hand.

However, this often has the opposite effect, undermining the strength of the relationship and keeping it from developing in a healthy way. Codependent people rarely realize that what they're doing is causing damage; they just think they're being helpful. If you think you might have a propensity for codependent relationships, you need to objectively consider it and decide if you're taking an undue burden upon yourself. You must be completely honest with yourself in your assessment. If you're unable to be sincere, you might want to consider seeking outside help.

First, consider whether you are having self-esteem issues. If you find that you don't value yourself as much as you should, especially when interacting with one or more of your relations, this is a red flag. The lack of self-worth might be buried deep down, so think long and hard. Think about current and past relationships of all kinds, with romantic interests and others. If you detect a pattern of low self-esteem and uneven devotion, then you've probably identified a codependent relationship. A pattern is important; isolated events are more likely to be simple relationship problems rather than a chronic psychological issue.

When looking to establish a pattern for codependent relationships, consider the following:

- Do you spend much more time caring for your relations than they do for you?
- Do you sacrifice and compromise on your own desires for the benefit of others?
- Do you feel personally responsible when unable to care for and help your partner?
- Do you feel more like a parent or guardian than an equal partner?
- Is it difficult to say no?

If you answer yes to three or more of these questions, you should seriously consider seeking group therapy or help from a professional counselor.

Codependent relationships can have serious long-term psychological effects, and damage your other relationships. It's important that you start valuing yourself and let others take responsibility for themselves. Codependency isn't easy to cure, but it's important to recognize and begin dealing with it sooner rather than later. Confronting the issue will inspire self-confidence, lead to healthier relationships, and bring a sense of inner peace you probably have not experienced in a while.

Why Do People Get Into Codependent Relationships?

To understand how codependent relationships form, it's important to know the characteristics of people who are predisposed to getting into them. Codependent tendencies often trace back to childhood, when we start to develop patterns in how we connect with people, or what psychologists call "attachment styles.

"The reason you develop an insecure attachment style is because you probably didn't have secure attachments with your parents,"

In codependent relationships, givers have anxious attachment styles—they define themselves by their relationship, and will do whatever it takes to stay in it. They make exceptions for anxiously attached people, however, because they get much more out of the relationship than they have to put in.

Givers and takers are drawn to each other — often subconsciously, says Daniels. Over time, givers wear themselves out as they fight for the reassurance they may never get from the taker, while the takers continue avoiding their emotions and taking responsibility for their actions.

Codependent Relationships - Are they Healthy?

They have a tendency to be the center of attention. They are also clingy and needy. They are in constant demand for getting love, attention, validation, and approval. But they are angry, blaming others for their actions, violent, critical, irritable, and/or emotionally unstable.

They are afraid of being controlled. They are resistant to their partner. They are also abusive to the giving partner in the relationship. If their partner confronts them about something, the taker could be in denial, they could be defensive, they could be procrastinators, they could rebel, they could be irresponsible, be indifferent, withdrawal from them completely, feel completely numb, or act incompetently. This person feels that the giver is responsible for validation and respect of their own feelings.

Caretakers are a bit different. They believe that they are responsible for their partner's feelings. They sacrifice a lot. They sacrifice their own needs, wants, and desires, to make everyone else happy. They give out of fear, not out of love.

Because of the lack of care on both parties, they will feel angry, resentful, trapped, unappreciated, disrespected, unloved, misunderstood, not validated, and frustrated. Any relationship headed in that direction will not last.

To overcome these types of relationships, we must value, validate, recognize, and understand ourselves. We need to love ourselves too. When we don't, we are only hurting ourselves.

Codependent relationships will always have problems. When one of these people leaves that relationship hoping that the next will be better, they come to realize that will run into the same problems. They will encounter anger, resentment, distance, lack of intimacy, frustration, unresolved baggage, excess baggage, boredom, lack of fulfillment and validation, and irritation amongst many other issues.

The way to reconcile this issue is to openly talk about the problems. Each party must take full responsibility for their actions and feelings. Each person needs to stop blaming the other person for his or her unhappiness. Be honest and own up to what you have done in the relationship. Learn that in most cases that you are not the victim of unhappiness. Essentially, you are the one that is causing your own unhappiness.

Remember you are the one that is responsible for your own happiness. If you want a healthy relationship, you are going to have to change!!!

Being Independent in a Codependent Relationship
People that are just starting off on their own or getting out of a codependent relationship may not think of being

independent as a natural feeling. The easiest way to become independent is to take small steps one at a time until it does become a natural feeling to you.

By following these simple steps you will soon be making great strides forward towards independence. It is important however that you take it slow and work on these steadily in order to ensure that you get the best results possible.

1. Pay Your Own Way: Nothing screams out the fact that you are dependent more than being a mooch type person. If letting someone treat you all of the time is normal to you whether it's your mom and dad or a boyfriend or girlfriend it might be tough to start paying for things yourself.

We all have bills that need to be paid with absolutely no exception. Things like the rent and utilities need to be paid in order to live period. You need to put these bills in your name so that you will be held responsible for them. If you decide to go see a movie or go out to dinner you need to pay for those activities as well.

2. Give Yourself Some Me Time: When you live at home or are in a relationship you constantly have company. If this is the case being alone all of the time may be a very strange feeling for you. Instead of trying to make sure that you are constantly surrounded by people why not try to get to know yourself instead.

You could do something as simple as just start reading more or pick a new hobby that you can do by yourself. This is going to help you figure out what you want personally and what you would like to get out of life.

3. Get Outside Your Comfort Zone: Being independent isn't easy. You are going to have to step out of your normal box for this.

Just because you are independent doesn't mean that you are going to live in solitude. You need to let go and have fun with your new self.

Codependent Problems in Relationships

Codependency causes serious pain and affects the majority of Americans, both in and out of relationships. There are all types of codependents, including caretakers, addicts, pleasers, and workaholics, to name a few. They all have one thing in common: They've lost the connection to their core. Their thoughts and behavior revolve around someone or something external, whether it's a person or an addiction.

It's as if they're turned inside out. Instead of self-esteem, they have other esteem, based upon what others think and feel. Instead of meeting their own needs, they meet the needs of others, and instead of responding to their own thoughts and feelings, they react to those of others. Hence, they have to control others to feel okay, but that just makes matters worse. It's a haywire system that leads to conflict and pain and makes emotional intimacy difficult.

Relationship Problems

Some people criticize the codependency movement and say that it's created more loneliness. They argue that relationships are nurturing and that we're naturally meant to be dependent. Codependents have problems receiving the good stuff that relationships can potentially offer. Many choose partners who are unhealthy.

Healing entails learning the differences between codependent and healthy interdependent relationships, between healthy caregiving and codependent caretaking, and understanding the boundaries between responsibility for yourself and responsibility to others, something that eludes codependents. Tools for recovery are all included in my book.

Not all codependents are caretakers, but if you are, you

have a hard time listening to other people's problems without trying to help, sometimes even feeling responsible and guilty for their feelings. This creates high reactivity and arguments of blame and guilt. Couples blame each other for their own feelings and defend themselves when their partner shares his or her feelings.

Boundaries and Intimacy

What's missing is a sense of separateness between them - called emotional boundaries - that your thoughts and feelings belong to you. "I'm not responsible for your feelings, and I didn't make you feel them." Weak boundaries make real intimacy difficult, if not impossible. For that to happen, you need to first have a sense of separate identity and feel safe enough to express your true feelings without feeling afraid of being criticized or rejected.

This is where the codependent core issue of low self-esteem comes in. When your sense of self is weak, you're afraid of rejection and abandonment, but on the flip-side, you fear losing yourself when you get attached in a relationship. You tend to give up your needs to accommodate your partner, sometimes letting go of outside friends and activities you used to enjoy. Even when your relationship isn't working, you feel stuck or trapped. Contrary to common belief, many codependents aren't even in relationships, because they're afraid of losing their independence.

If you're dating, you might have to dance a tightrope of pursuing partners, but never really a commitment, or distancing yourself, but never really leaving. It's a two-step that's even done in marriages but creates constant pain in the relationships, highlighted by fleeting moments of closeness - just enough to keep the dance going. Some couples give up on intimacy entirely.

Communication

Codependents have a dilemma. If you can't say "No"

37

without feeling guilty, you end up resentful from agreeing to things you rather not. Due to fears of rejection, you avoid taking positions at all costs - like a clever politician, you're indirect and don't want to say anything that might upset someone else. Additionally, due to guilt and low self-esteem, codependents are always explaining and justifying themselves.

Improving your communication by learning how to be assertive, how to set boundaries, and how to handle verbal abuse is a vital part of recovery.

Start Healing

Codependents spend their precious lives worrying about things and people over which they have no control. Healing from codependency starts with getting to know yourself better, honoring yourself, and expressing yourself.

Here are some tips:
- Practice on saying "No." Remember, "No" is a complete sentence.
- When someone tells you a problem, just listen. Say, "I understand. That's a real problem." Period!
- Identify your feelings throughout the day. Journal and share them.
- When you don't feel great, ask yourself what you need. Try to meet that need, and reach out if necessary.
- Do things that make you happy. Don't wait for someone else.
- Building a relationship with yourself leaves you no time to worry about someone you can't control. That's how you heal codependency.

How to Be Aware That You're in a Codependent Relationship and What You Can Do About It

You know that your spouse has a problem and needs your help and support. And you have always prided yourself on being there for him. But now you have come to realize that maybe this isn't a good thing. Maybe you have become dependent on his need of you?

Codependence just used to refer to those linked to alcoholism or drug abuse sufferers. However, today's psychologists have a broader definition. "It really is about unhealthy emotional people can be obsessed with the pain and suffering of the other person dependencies".

Six signs you are in a codependent relationship

So are you a codependent? How can you tell? Here are six signs that might suggest you are in a codependent relationship.

1. Do you become obsessed with fixing and rescuing needy people? Codependents are more oriented to other people's reality than their own; they want to be someone else's savior which makes them feel happier about themselves.

2. Are you easily absorbed in the pain and problems of other people?

3. Are you trying to control someone? Is someone trying to control you? Neediness is a hallmark of a codependent relationship. One person's happiness depends on having the other person right there - right now. Not letting you hang out with friends, calling frequently to check up on you, having to be with you all the time - these are controlling behaviors

4. Do you do more than your share -- all of the time? Many codependent people were the favorite child because they did more - took care of the sick parent, got straight A's, cleaned the house. However, as an adult, when this behavior is carried on it can result in that person feeling like a martyr, victimized by doing it all.

5. Are you always seeking approval and recognition? Low-self esteem is a mark of codependence. A codependent person judges themselves harshly; they have difficulty asking others to meet their needs and they don't believe they are

worthwhile or lovable.

6. Would you do anything to hold on to a relationship? Do you fear being abandoned? Many adults in codependent relationships come from families where they felt unloved or were abandoned by either one parent or both. This makes them willing to put up with a lot in order to keep their partner with them.

Reading the signs, you think you may be in a codependent relationship, so now what? Should you leave? Get counseling? It is hard to think of yourself and your needs after focusing on your spouse's needs for so long and fitting yourself around their issues, their demands, their moods. But it is time to put yourself back in the center, take control and think about what is good for you.

For Men - 11 Signs You're in a Codependent Relationship - And How to Get Out

It's often obvious that a needy, demanding woman who clings to a man has codependent tendencies. However, a relationship consists of two people, and HE is no less responsible. In fact, his behavior can also be labeled "codependent." Two people who have codependent tendencies may act in opposite ways: While one is needy and drains her partner, the other may have an enlarged sense of responsibility to his partner and is overly sensitive to her needs and demands.

In fact, people with opposing codependent styles tend to attract each other. These opposing psychological profiles have been termed "takers" and "caretakers."

Codependent relationships are complicated, and they're often characterized by manipulation, lack of boundaries, repressed emotions, emotional volatility, jealousy

issues, verbal abuse, etc. Both partners tend to have complicated back-stories, which often serve to justify abnormal behavior. If you're a man feeling stuck in a codependent relationship, realize that your happiness is worth the effort it takes to move on.

First, take a look at this list, which identifies just some of the signs to look for:
- You feel that you're responsible for her, and it's your job to make her happy and solve her problems
- You suppress your emotions and avoid confrontation
- You have the sense of sacrificing the life you want so that you can be with her and take care of her
- You feel trapped at times, and have the sense that you are planning an eventual escape
- You feel tremendous guilt at the thought of abandoning her
- She is extremely jealous and makes it difficult for you to interact with other females or have female friends
- She has an intense fear of rejection and abandonment
- She lives her life in a way that depends on you for many of her needs, as opposed to being independent and having a variety of fulfilling relationships
- She has expressed that she wouldn't be able to live her life if you betrayed or abandoned her
- She depends almost exclusively on you as her source of happiness and validation
- She dominates and manipulates you through her emotional response, which is often too extreme

These are just some of the signs that are easiest to spot from the man's point of you view. If you feel that you may be in a codependent relationship, or you feel as if you're trapped and there's no way out, most like. Being in a codependent relationship makes for a stressful and unhappy lifestyle. And yet, your avoidant tendencies may keep you from following through with a break-up or separation.

You may be planning to break up for a long time, but you just keep holding off -- many men wait years, or even a lifetime, remaining in such a relationship. It's important that you don't dwell on planning, and you take certain actions, fast. If you feel ready to begin the separation process, DO NOT hesitate: The longer you wait, and the more time you both invest, the more difficult it becomes.

You may want to consider getting the help of a counselor. Be sure that the counselor doesn't assume that you want to maintain the relationship if you're choosing to move on; many counselors operate from the assumption that the relationship should be "fixed."

Finally, many men are in dire need of a map that:
- Identifies what is dysfunctional in your relationship
- Affirms your right to leave an unhappy relationship
- Guides you through the break up in a way that minimizes pain and hardship for you both

2.2 Three Ways To Overcome Codependent Relationships

Of all relationships, codependent relationships are probably the least healthy ones. If you happen to be in one of these relationships you should quickly figure out how to solve the issue of codependency or simply call it quits. Whether you are codependent or she is, if the problem is left unsolved, it's going to have negative consequences on you and her in the future.

Below are three ways to overcome codependent relationships.

1. Therapy/Counseling

If you have the financial means, this is probably the best solution. Having professional help is the fastest and most effective way to finding out why has your relationship become codependent and what needs to be done in order for you and her to go back to those wonderful times you had at the beginning of the relationship. It is also important to note that professional help is unbiased compared to a relative or close friend. A more familiar person will think of what's best for you not for the couple while the professional will consider both parties' interest in the issue at hand.

2.   Let Her Know What's Wrong

Everyone has needs and those needs need to be satisfied. At some point not expressing your needs or feelings will lead to a bigger need of attention which will eventually lead to selfishness. Selfishness is one of the main symptoms in codependent relationships. One of the partner feels the other one should drive all their attention towards them which is not healthy for both partners. Talking about it is the easiest way out of it so don't hesitate to communicate your needs to your partner. After all, if she wasn't interested in making you happy then you need to ask yourself why she's with you.

3.   Participate In Different Activities

This may sound controversial but believe it or not, some activities are better done alone. Usually, things are better done in pairs but if it's making you and your partner uncomfortable it's time to switch it up a little. For example, training sessions, girls night out, boys night out, basically any activity you would do better without your partner around. Why? It'll give you the opportunity to meet new people and sometimes it's all it takes to make you or her realize how dependent you've become and how you or her need to change.

When it comes to relationships, the drama is inevitable. You can't predict when something will go wrong in the beginning because you seem to be in heaven. However, if you end up in one of those bad relationships there are very few options for you to choose. Should you try and resolve the issue or move on? One thing's for sure, if it's one of those codependent relationships, you may want to opt for a solution as soon as possible since it can only get worse from this point on.

CHAPTER 3

ARE YOU A CAREGIVER OR CODEPENDENT CARETAKER?

Conventional belief is that we can never love too much, but that isn't always true. Sometimes, love can blind us so that we deny painful truths. We might believe broken promises and continue to excuse someone's abuse or rejection. We may empathize with them but not enough with ourselves. If we grew up in a troubled environment, we might confuse our pain with love. Although relationships have disappointments and conflicts, love isn't supposed to be painful and hurt so much. As codependents, we have a habit of ignoring our needs and constantly putting those of others first. We end up self-sacrificing. By not having boundaries, we harm ourselves and the relationship. We might also confuse love with being someone's caretaker.

Caretaking vs. Caregiving
Parental love is expected to be unconditional and one-sided toward their young children. As they grow, good parenting includes mutual respect for each others' boundaries. Caregiving is a normal outgrowth of love and is also part of healthy adult relationships. When someone we love is in need, we naturally want to help. Yet there's a

44

difference between "caregiving" and codependent "caretaking." In the latter situation, we might care for someone in a manner that is intrusive or enabling. We do harm to the other person and risk sacrificing our own lives in the process.

With codependent caretaking, often there's more "taking" than giving. The caretaker's objectives can subtlety take precedence. This is because caregiving comes from abundance, and caretaking emanates from need and deprivation. Caretaking can become so habitual that it enables and disables the recipient so that he or she doesn't take responsibility for his or her behavior and needs. It treats that person like a child who doesn't have to grow up and reinforces his or her lack of confidence. Again, due to the lack of boundaries, caretaking eventually negatively impacts the relationship as a whole.

When one partner acts as a caretaker of the other, it creates an imbalance and unhealthy mutual dependency – codependence. The caretaker doesn't have to be as vulnerable as his or her partner. The caretaker feels needed and superior and at the same time is assured that his or her partner won't leave. Over time, both end up feeling guilty and angry. The more a caretaker becomes invested in the problems of his or her partner, the more that advice and control characterize the dynamic between them. What may have started out as an act of love devolves into resentment when well-meaning advice or wisdom isn't followed.

So how can you tell the difference between caregiving and caretaking? Here are some of the differences:

Caretaker
- Sacrifices self-righteous about own opinions
- Helping is compulsive
- Feels responsible for others
- Crosses boundaries with unsolicited advice
- Is judgmental

- Knows what's best for others
- Gives with strings attached or expectations
- Feels exhausted, irritated, frustrated, anxious
- Feels unappreciated or resentful
- Discourages others from thinking for themselves
- Uses nonassertive, pushy, judging, "you" statements
- Tries to control recipient

Caregiver
- Practices self-care
- Respects others' opinions
- Helping is volitional
- Feels responsible for self and to others
- Respect boundaries. Waits to be asked for advice
- Feels love and empathy
- Knows what's best for self
- Gives freely without expectations
- Feels energized
- Doesn't take others' actions personally
- Encourages others to solve their own problems
- Uses assertive "I" statements
- Supports recipient
- Learn to Detach with Love

The challenge of change is learning to detach and let go. That doesn't mean we care any less about our loved ones, but we allow them the dignity of making mistakes and finding their own way. We take care of our own needs that we may be neglecting, and we empower others to do the same by supporting their choices. That also means we empathically and lovingly allow them to suffer the resulting consequences, by not removing the natural consequences of their actions, nor having an "I told you so" attitude.

Make "Live and let live" your mantra, and practice saying things like:
- "I'm so sorry to hear about your situation."

46

- "You really have a dilemma."
- What are your options?"
- What decision (actions) are you leaning toward?" or "What does your gut tell you?"
- "Trust your instincts."
- "I'm sure you'll find a solution."
- "I believe you can handle it."

Watching those you love struggle can be very difficult, and it can take all your strength not to jump in and help, especially when others expect you to behave in the old way. They'll likely try to reel you in to give advice and other help. Because caretaking can be a compulsion, you may need outside support to maintain your boundaries and be overwhelmed with guilt. Detachment doesn't mean being emotionally cold but taking a hands-off – ego-off approach. This is truly loving someone. Your guilt will lessen in time and with it resentment making for a better relationship.

CHAPTER 4

MANAGING CODEPENDENT RELATIONSHIPS

Codependent relationships can range from the annoying to the truly scary, dependent upon how the codependency is ultimately expressed. Codependency may be a symptom of deeper issues that need resolution or it may simply be an infantile attempt to win love. In either case, managing codependent relationships can be a significant problem.

The term "codependent" or "co-dependent" is thrown around fairly easily nowadays in order to describe all manner of annoying companions. But what is a codependent? A codependent is a person with low self-esteem who feels the need to be loved by others and will do anything to stay in a relationship, relying on the other person to make them feel worthy. The codependent often attempts to win this love by doing things or giving gifts to the object of their affection. Ultimately, when these gestures are spurned, the codependent is hurt and responds with sadness, frustration, anger -- and guilt.

Codependents are, by definition, manipulators. They may be fairly innocent, low-grade manipulators, or they may be burgeoning world-dominating evil geniuses, but they are all manipulators. If you are dealing with codependent

48

relationships, it is fundamental to understand this aspect before moving forward. The cardinal rule of managing codependent relationships is this: You must cut the manipulative, codependent behavior off the cold.

The only real cure for codependency is for the codependent to find a source of genuine self-esteem. This involves cultivating a competence in which they may take pride and, as a result, it can be a long path towards good, well balanced mental health. As a friend of a codependent you may assist them on this path, but doing so without enabling their codependent behaviors is difficult.

Here are a few pointers to assist in managing codependent relationships:

1.   Cut off the Codependent Behavior - This must be handled on an individual basis, depending upon the personality of the codependent, but it comes down to not rewarding codependent behaviors. Do not accept the gifts or the offers of over-the-top assistance. The seemingly loving gestures are a bait to attract your affection and a return favor, so you must not reward that.

2.   Encourage the Codependent to Cultivate a Hobby - The codependent needs to find an area of authentic expertise in which he or she can take pride and this may be in the form of a hobby or the study of a field of particular interest. If they already enjoy dancing, encourage them to take lessons, or if they show an interest in model railroading, encourage them to build a layout. Creative outlets can be tremendous channels for the codependent's energies and they help to build that necessary self-esteem.

3.   Encourage the Codependent to Advance at Work - Often the codependent personality will be bored with their work and they redirect their focus inappropriately. Encourage them to seek additional challenges or

specializations through their work. Or, if their current job is truly dead-end, encourage them to polish their resume and seek better employment elsewhere. This, again, is a huge self-esteem builder and that is what the codependent needs the most.

Managing codependent relationships can be a nightmare, especially for those who truly care about the person. Ultimately the burden falls on them to either kick the codependent out of their lives altogether or to try to give the codependent the firm support that they need.

What Should You Do if You're in a Codependent Relationship?

If you've noticed traits of codependency in your relationship. Through therapy, codependent relationships can become more balanced and fulfilling—but both parties need to be committed to making the relationship work.

The anxiously attached partner shouldn't let the fear of losing his or her loved one prevent the suggestion of professional help. "It's important to take that risk anyway, "If that person is going to run away, they're going to run away anyway." People in codependent relationships aren't bad people.

How to Tell if You're Codependent

If you are in a relationship that you think may be codependent, the first step to independence is to stop looking at the other and take a look at yourself.

• If you honestly say that you agree with the following statements, you may be codependent.

• You tend to love people that you can pity and rescue.

• You feel responsible for the actions of others.

• You do more than your share in the relationship to keep the peace.

• You are afraid of being abandoned or alone.

• You feel responsible for your partner's happiness.

- You need approval from others to gain your own self-worth.
- You have difficulty adjusting to change.
- You have difficulty making decisions and often doubt yourself.
- You are reluctant to trust others.
- Your moods are controlled by the thoughts and feelings of those around you.

Codependency is often seen in people with borderline personality disorder (BPD), although this does not mean all people with codependency issues also meet the criteria for a diagnosis of BPD.

The Relationship Between Codependency and Addiction

One of the many problems with a codependent relationship is that you may be inadvertently enabling a partner's addiction. In your attempt to show your love by "helping" your partner, you can discourage him or her from seeking the treatment necessary to get sober.

For example:

- You justify your husband's drinking by saying he has had a stressful day or needs to relax.
- You make excuses when your girlfriend can't come to social functions because she is under the influence of heroin.
- You let your boyfriend borrow your prescription opioids whenever he complains of any minor discomfort, even though you're worried about his growing dependence on the medication.
- You quietly take on extra responsibilities around the house or in parenting your children because your partner is always under the influence.
- You find yourself frequently apologizing to others or doing favors to repair relationships damaged by your partner's drug or alcohol abuse.
- You risk your own financial future by loaning money

to your partner to cover debts incurred from substance abuse.

Addiction impairs judgment and critical thinking skills. This makes it very difficult for someone with a substance use disorder to see that he or she needs help. When you go out of your way to prevent your partner from experiencing the consequences of substance abuse, you make it less likely that he or she will acknowledge that a problem exists.

Loving someone with a substance use disorder can also cause your codependent tendencies to spiral out of control. When your partner is behaving erratically due to drug or alcohol abuse, it's easy to resort to using codependent behavior in your fight to maintain a sense of control over chaotic surroundings. This creates a vicious cycle that traps both of you in a dysfunctional and unhealthy relationship.

Healing from Codependency

The good news is that codependency is a learned behavior, which means it can be unlearned. If you love your partner and want to keep the relationship, you need to heal yourself first and foremost.

Some healthy steps to healing your relationship from codependency include:

1.   Start being honest with yourself and your partner. Doing things that we do not want to do not only waste our time and energy, but it also brings on resentments. Saying things that we do not mean only hurts us because we then are living a lie. Be honest in your communication and in expressing your needs and desires.

2.   Stop negative thinking. Catch yourself when you begin to think negatively. If you begin to think that you deserve to be treated badly, catch yourself and change your thoughts. Be positive and have higher expectations.

3.   Don't take things personally. It takes a lot of work for a codependent person not to take things personally,

especially when in an intimate relationship. Accepting the other as they are without trying to fix or change them is the first step.

4.   Take breaks. There is nothing wrong with taking a break from your partner. It is healthy to have friendships outside of your partnership. Going out with friends brings us back to our center, reminding us of who we really are.

5.   Consider counseling. Get into counseling with your partner. A counselor serves as an unbiased third party. They can point out codependent tendencies and actions between the two of you that you may not be aware of. Feedback can provide a starting point and direction. Change cannot happen if we do not change.

Rely on peer support. Co-Dependents Anonymous is a 12-step group similar to Alcoholics Anonymous that helps people who want to break free of their codependent behavior patterns.

Establish boundaries. Those who struggle with codependency often have trouble with boundaries. We do not know where our needs begin or where the other's end. We often thrive off guilt and feel bad when we do not put the other first.

How Can You Tell if you're In a Codependent Relationship?

One question you should ask yourself is: how much time in a given day do you spend thinking about your relationship? If the answer is most of the time, Daniels says your relationship is probably codependent. Also, if you are constantly seeking reassurance, asking questions like, "Do you love me? " and "Do you promise you won't leave me?" you may be codependent,

Other signs of codependency include putting your partner on a pedestal, idealizing that person despite his or her faults and making excuses for your loved one when he or she neglects important tasks. Givers often think they're helping their partners when in reality they're actually preventing them from personal growth. And if one partner in your

53

relationship has an addiction, it's much more likely to become codependent.

One partner's addiction to alcohol or drugs can take a toll on both partners and can cause more imbalances in the relationship. "So can addiction to money, ego, power, lying, or love, and sex," Beattie says. The person with the addiction can neglect his or her partner in the process, while the other may feel the need to give more to that person out of fear, guilt, or habit, according to Beattie.

It's important to take note of the signs, as codependent relationships can often mimic healthy relationships at first. As time passes, givers become laden with their responsibilities to the takers, and takers become overwhelmed by the giver's emotional neediness. Without changing course, the relationship will ultimately become unhappy and unsustainable.

Why Codependent Relationships Form

What causes us to seek out these types of relationships? "As far as givers go, available research suggests that emotional abuse and neglect put us at risk for codependence, If you learned that the only way to connect with a difficult parent was to subordinate your own needs and cater to theirs, then you may be set up for similar relationships throughout your life."

Weiss says the term codependence stems from something called "trauma theory," which implies a traumatic event, sometimes occurring during formative years, possibly caused by violence or some other form of violation.

You may also have beliefs or personality traits that make it easier to fall into a codependent relationship. "You can over-internalize religious or cultural values that prescribe self-sacrifice for others.

Can the Relationship Be Saved?

You might indeed be able to salvage a codependent relationship without going back to being codependent. You

54

can't do it alone. The other person must do their part as well. The goal is to have an interdependent relationship in which both people give something to the relationship and also benefit from the relationship.

Changing a codependent relationship is no easy task. A counselor can guide you through the process as you both learn new ways of thinking and behaving. You can have some effect simply by acting in ways that aren't codependent. Yet, if the other person's actions show that they aren't interested in a healthy relationship, at some point you will need to decide if staying in that situation is beneficial for your mental health.

Overcoming Codependency Relationship

The first step in getting things back on track is to understand the meaning of a codependent relationship. Experts say it's a pattern of behavior in which you find yourself dependent on approval from someone else for your self-worth and identity.

One key sign is when your sense of purpose in life wraps around making extreme sacrifices to satisfy your partner's needs.

"Codependent relationships signify a degree of unhealthy clinginess, where one person doesn't have self-sufficiency or autonomy," says Scott Wetzler, Ph.D., psychology division chief at Albert Einstein College of Medicine. "One or both parties depend on their loved ones for fulfillment."

Anyone can become codependent. Some research suggests that people who have parents who emotionally abused or neglected them in their teens are more likely to enter codependent relationships

For many people, pain is what they know. Conflict is comfortable. Dealing with an unavailable, distant, or inappropriate partner is their wheelhouse. A partner who wants nothing more than to be with them and make them a top priority is alien.

Many people stay in self-defeating relationships too long

because they are fearful of being alone or feel responsible for their partner's happiness. They may say they want out -- but they end up staying. Others may leave but repeat the same or a similar self-destructive pattern in a new relationship. The adrenaline rush that they experience when they feel passionate toward someone can be addictive. For many people, the reason behind excessive emotional reliance on a partner is co-dependency -- a tendency to put other's needs before their own.

So what can you do if you are paralyzed by fear or unable to risk leaving a relationship that is unhealthy for you? First, you need to acknowledge it. Fear doesn't go away by itself -- it tends to morph into something else. If you sometimes find that you sabotage your own needs in relationships, there could be many reasons. However, codependency symptoms are common for people who grew up in a dysfunctional home -- especially if you took on the role of a caretaker.

Many people fear getting hurt emotionally and might flee a healthy relationship or engage in some form of self-protective behavior by staying in an unhealthy one. For many people, pain is what they know. Conflict is comfortable. Dealing with an unavailable, distant, or inappropriate partner is their wheelhouse. A partner who wants nothing more than to be with them and make them a top priority is alien.

Do you find yourself falling into one or more of these codependent relationship patterns?

• People pleasing: You go above and beyond to make others happy. You might avoid confronting your partner about important issues because you fear rejection or worry more about a partner's feelings than your own.

• Define your self-worth by others: Do you care too much about what others think of you?

• Ignore red flags: Do you ignore a partner's dishonesty, possessiveness, or jealous tendencies?

• Give too much in a relationship: You might even ignore your own self-care or feel that you're being selfish if

56

you take care of yourself.

•   Have poor boundaries: This can' mean you have trouble saying "no" to the requests of others or allow others to take advantage of you.

•   Stay in a relationship with someone who is distant, unavailable, or abusive - even though you know deep down inside that they may never meet your emotional needs.

Steps to Reclaiming Healthy Love in Your Life:

•   Visualize yourself in a loving relationship that meets your needs. If your current relationship is destructive, look at ways you self-sabotage and examine your own behaviors.

•   Challenge your beliefs and self-defeating thoughts about your self-worth. You don't need to prove anything to another person about your worth.

•   Notice your negative self-judgments. Be kind and compassionate toward yourself.

•   Remind yourself daily that it's healthy to accept help from others and a sign of strength rather than weakness. Counseling, friendships, and online resources can be tremendously helpful in supporting you in your journey of finding a happy relationship.

•   Don't let your fear of rejection stop you from achieving loving, intimate relationships. Surrender your shield and let others in.

Take a moment to consider that you might be hooked on the feeling that being in love brings pain. If so, you might be self-sabotaging your chances of having a healthy relationship where you can get your needs met.

4.2   5 Steps to Loving Yourself and Living Happily Ever After

We are conditioned to feel crap about ourselves. You

never hear people say "Yes, I think I'm great!" or "I love that about myself, I think it's really cool," or "I just really make myself laugh.".

It just sounds a bit weird that it's more socially acceptable to mock yourself, put yourself down and bemoan your shortcomings. It's almost cool to appear to be broken, dysfunctional and miserable.

The trouble is that we're forced to conform to other people's ideas of what we should be rather than be accepted for who we really are.

We're spat out of school after being shoehorned into categories and graded like goods on a factory production line. And then, as adults, our insecurities drive advertisers to constantly prey on our self-loathing. We're continually led to believe that we're too fat, too stupid, too short, too insecure, too lazy and too unproductive. We constantly compare ourselves to others and consistently find ourselves inadequate.

As adults, we continue to feel like children being told off for being too slow or too messy or not trying our best. Rather than it being our parents or teachers putting us down, we let others do it — the media, our bosses, friends and even more destructively, ourselves. We never stop bemoaning ourselves to the point that we allow those negative voices to cause us misery and permeate our whole lives. Part of true mature thinking is to own and deal with these thoughts. You need to take control of the ones that are valid and to own constructive criticism.

It was Mark Twain who said: "The worst loneliness is not to be comfortable with yourself.".

And, he was right. You will spend your whole life with yourself. The quality of your relationship with yourself will have a direct bearing on the quality of your life as a whole. It's probably a strange thought that you are in a relationship with yourself. For many people, they are themselves and, in a haze of introspective emotion, they can't see beyond a two-dimensional representation of their existence. It's a childish state that many of us remain locked into.

But, to really develop, you need to separate from yourself, develop some sense of objectivity and become your own best friend. You have to distance the childish voices and impulses and to cultivate a mature view of yourself. You need to be able to look down at yourself with compassion and ultimately love and care for yourself. Having the inner strength to talk yourself through things, the capacity to self-soothe, to be entertained by yourself and to find yourself interesting is incredibly powerful. To be able to look after yourself, respect your own point of view and be confident in your own thinking is liberating and empowering.

So, what are the steps to loving yourself?

1.   Learn to love yourself from the outside – become your own best friend

Try to remove yourself from your immediate emotion and look at yourself objectively. Of course, we all need to feel emotions and be in the moment. But, being able to separate from them and simultaneously retain a sense of balanced objectivity is a valuable skill.

Sometimes we get so involved with our inner feelings that we can't make progress. Strong emotions can cloud your judgment and having a two-dimensional sense of yourself where you are with your emotions is often detrimental to your well-being. Become your own best friend. Recognize your emotions and try to nurture a loving and supporting view of yourself so that you can give pieces of advice and comments that are parallel with your inner self.

This sounds more complicated than it actually is. But, think of it this way:

•   We all have a feeling side and a thinking side and it's just a case of recognizing and synchronizing the two to work harmoniously.

•   There are a number of ways to develop this way of supportive thinking. Daily journaling or keeping a diary is a good start as it helps you to reflect on the day's events.

Spending five minutes a day on reflective writing can kickstart your inner voice and allow you access to an inner dialogue that will comfort and support you.

• Once you have a sense of your inner voice, nurture and develop it. Converse with it and talk to it. Having an inner dialogue can bring you closer to yourself.

2.   Spend time alone and learn to enjoy your own company

How often do you actively do things alone? There's always a pressure to be seen with other people or to feel as if we are "Billy no mates". However, spending quality time with yourself is extremely valuable and underrated.

So many people seem terrified of themselves and clearly don't like being alone and can't stand their own company. They constantly fill every waking moment with entertainment and chatter to avoid confronting themselves. To them, a moment alone in contemplation would be a horror.

But, you can't avoid yourself. It's impossible and the sooner you learn to love your own company, the better. As with any relationship, it takes time and effort to make it work. There may well be times when you drive yourself nuts but also times when you start to find inner peace and acceptance that's priceless.

Have a go at simply scheduling a time to do stuff on your own. You can try going for a walk, shopping, going to the cinema or a concert. Even allowing yourself to daydream, sitting with your eyes closed and listening to music is a great way to spend quality time with yourself.

Maybe meditation would work well for you. Any activity that allows you to concentrate on your inner thoughts and feelings is valuable in nurturing your inner relationship.

3.   Develop self-acceptance and compassion

We all instinctively spend a lot of our time comparing ourselves to other people. We are actively encouraged to do this at school and work and our performance is constantly scrutinized. On social media and in advertising, we are incessantly bombarded with images and ideas about how we should be. There's little wonder that so many of us are full of self-loathing and feel inadequate.

In the past, we were only able to compare ourselves to people within a much smaller demographic. We didn't have access to media, the internet, and travel, so we were able to see ourselves a little more objectively.

Today, the context is essentially the whole world. Inevitably, we are exposed to the best of everything — the fastest, tallest, slimmest, most beautiful, best designed, most efficient or most stylish. It's hopeless and demoralizing trying to compete with all of those.

We need to stop comparing ourselves to others. That's not to say that we can't have aspirations and dreams for development. However, learning to love our individuality is one of the most important steps to loving yourself. There's little point in looking at what other people have or haven't got. There will always be someone who is better and worse than you.

We need to learn to measure and celebrate our progress in terms of our own personal achievement. What really matters is that we are slightly better today than we were yesterday and not that we are better than someone else. Comparing ourselves to others ultimately erodes our self-confidence and kills our self-esteem. By all means, be ruthlessly competitive with yourself.

If we can learn to cut ourselves a bit of slack and accept that life is going to be a bit rubbish sometimes, then we will find that we'll be much happier and much more accepting of your own limitations.

4.   Find your flow activity

All people have a gift or a skill that they are better at than others. It can be something that they love or something that gives them enormous satisfaction and pleasure. Sometimes, it feels so good that it's almost like a guilty pleasure. When our brains are in what's called "in flow", we are in one of the most satisfying and fulfilling states that the human mind can be in.

Sadly, many people go through life without finding their flow activities. They never get to spend that quality time developing their skill, feeling positive about their achievement and being one with their purpose in life. If you don't know what your flow activities are, then think about the last time you lost track of the time of day. It's when you got so absorbed in doing something that nothing else mattered. You were just happy and at peace with yourself.

These activities are fundamentally precious to your personal well-being so you should schedule more time doing them.

5. Care for your mind and body

Ultimately, learning to live with and love yourself is about respect and taking the time to listen to your inner voice. It's incredibly hard to attune yourself to the depths of your inner workings if your outer layers aren't being looked after properly. This makes it important to look after your physical well-being, too.

Starting to make positive choices about food and exercise can have far-reaching effects on your mood and happiness. Just by being proactive about healthy eating, making informed choices, and respecting your body is a mindset that can spill over into other aspects of your life. Keep in mind that there is an incredibly strong link between physical and mental health.

If everything above just seems far too difficult and complicated, start by simply taking control of your body. Learn to care for your physical health more fully. Start to exercise and be deliberate in your eating habits. Small changes can have a big impact. The very act of deciding to take care and to regain physical control can have positive repercussions way beyond those small first steps.

The bottom line is that you are the only person

responsible for your life. You can't escape yourself. It's the one relationship that you can't break off. You can't divorce yourself, sack yourself or dump yourself. However, you can reinvent yourself so you can become better and stronger. You are stuck with yourself for life and the sooner you come to accept, love and respect yourself, the happier and more fulfilling your life will be.

4.3   Does Codependence Run In Your Family?

One way that dysfunctional helping and giving are probably "inherited" is through observational learning (though our genetic inheritance may also influence personality traits, like empathy, associated with dysfunctional helping and giving). The basic idea is that people often learn how to act by observing the behavior of another (a "model") rather than through direct experience. Indeed, quite a bit of research finds that parents' helping behavior, and what they say about helping, influences the helping of their children, even when those children become adults. Although what models do might be a bit more important than what they say about helping, apparently both are important.

In short, growing up watching important adults over-help, rescue, and enable, makes us more prone to it ourselves, especially if we identify with those adults and hear them exalted by others as saintly for all they put up with. These behavioral scripts are usually learned unconsciously when we are too young to understand or have access to their negative consequences. Instead, we just learn that in this situation this is what people do. Dysfunctional helping becomes familiar and routine, despite its hazards. Because these patterns often repeat without awareness, family therapy is sometimes necessary for identifying and breaking them.

This means that one of the most important things we can do is clean up our own codependent act for the sake of our (grand) children, making sure that our youngsters don't grow up watching us provide "helpful" accommodations that make it easier for others to maintain addictions, be irresponsible, underperforming, or unhealthy, etc. You don't want to model that "good" and responsible people sacrifice themselves to care for under-functioning others whose need for help is manufactured by their own poor choices. You need to show them and tell them that loving someone and being a good person doesn't mean accepting imbalanced relationships and allowing others to take advantage of you. You have to teach them, verbally and through example, that once it's obvious our help and giving has fostered dependence, irresponsibility, incompetence, harmed our relationships, or led us to feel disrespected or taken advantage of, we should call the deal off and save our resources, nurturing, and support for people that will use our assistance to move forward with their lives.

Codependence involves relationship patterns characterized by imbalanced giving and receiving where relationship intimacy and closeness are built on one's person's ongoing crisis and the other's rescuing and enabling. We have to make sure this isn't the model we provide to our youngsters with our own relationships. Instead, we have to show (and tell) them that satisfying intimate relationships are equitable over time and that mutual caring and giving builds healthy intimacy.

People prone to codependent relationships are often very empathic so it makes sense that you might teach your (grand) child to manage their empathy so it doesn't set them up for trouble. Teach them verbally and through an example to step back and think it through before impulsively helping or giving. It can be hard to watch someone suffer the consequences of their irresponsible actions but to assume those for them (for example, by bailing them out or covering for them) is to interfere with their learning of important life lessons.

People prone to codependent relationships usually have

low self-esteem. Sometimes they doubt that people will want to be in a relationship with them unless they give more than they receive. People with low self-esteem are also more easily manipulated into enabling "takers" and people in the throes of addiction. Sometimes people with low self-esteem boost their self-esteem by helping low-functioning others who, by comparison, make them feel capable and competent. If you can, redirect their helpful tendencies to animals, people, and causes that will truly benefit from their help. This is a more stable and satisfying source of self-esteem and a less troublesome helping path.

Low self-esteem usually results from parental absence, indifference, or neglect, which suggests to a child they are fundamentally not of value. In families with long-standing codependence patterns, a parents' codependent relationship with another child or adult can also lead a child to feel unloved and unlovable, setting them up for future codependence, or for their own poor functioning (since that appears to be the route to receiving love and care). Promote healthy self-esteem in your youngsters by telling them they are loved, by prioritizing your relationships with them, paying them attention, supporting their interests, and providing consistent and loving attention to their needs. Show them you care about them and their future by using positive disciplinary methods rather than shame-based methods that make them feel like they are bad people when they mess up (being too permissive is almost as bad since it can send a message that you don't care enough to bother or think they're hopeless).

You and your loved ones may need to seek professional help. Breaking family codependence patterns sometimes requires family and individual therapy to address the self-esteem and attachment issues that make codependence more likely to occur.

4.4 Avoid Getting Burnt In A Codependency Relationship

65

It can sometimes be difficult to tell the difference between devotion and addiction. Such is the case for codependency relationships. In these relationships, one member is so desperate for acceptance, attention, and love that they literally become emotionally "codependent."

Codependency relationships are a common problem and have been for ages. They commonly arise with people that had difficult relationships growing up. Children are very impressionable and can have a tendency to blame themselves for problems since their worlds are so self-centric. If they suffer from relationship problems early in life, the unhealthy thought processes and perceptions can eventually cause self-destructive habits. A rough rejection by a romantic interest, abuse from a family member, or loss of a friend often leads to codependency relationships in the future.

If you're concerned you might have an issue with codependency, make haste in getting to the bottom of it. You may want to take our codependency quiz at the bottom of this article. Codependents often suffer from a variety of mental issues, from OCD to high stress to low self-esteem. Eventually, these psychological effects will take their toll on physical health as well. In addition, codependency relationships tend to involve violence and turmoil. Because of these dangerous side effects, codependents should seek help as soon as possible.

The first step is admitting that you may indeed have an issue. If you're unsure whether you're in an unhealthy relationship, there are some telling signs to look for. For instance, do you always feel like you need to have the situation under control? Do you worry over little details and try to make everything perfect for your partner? This shows an extreme devotion to your partner's happiness, and is a potential sign of codependency, especially if the partner doesn't reciprocate.

Codependents often feel locked up in their relationships, with no way out. A long history of awkward relationships and difficulty with opening up to people is another strong sign. Finally, do you frequently find yourself compromising on your beliefs, desires and needs to please your partner? Are you more worried about their happiness than your own well-being? Do you avoid taking a stand or confronting them in fear of a backlash? These are the most telling signs and strongly indicate an addiction.

Don't worry if some of these might apply to you. Just because some of these seem to ring true doesn't mean you have a psychological disorder. It might just be a relationship problem, or you might just be worrying too much. For additional help, feel free to check out our codependency relationships quiz for a more in-depth personality test.

If you do think you're codependent, you should consider consulting a therapist or finding group therapy through groups like Codependent Anonymous. Many people are in some kind of codependency relationships, and a well-trained counselor will be able to identify and help you deal with it. It's better to be safe than sorry in cases like this. Obsessive love isn't loving at all. If you care for yourself and your relationships, you won't tolerate the corruptive effects of codependency relationships.

CHAPTER 5

CODEPENDENCY AND ADDICTION

Men who are addicts are also codependent. Their lives revolve around their addiction - whether it's a drug (including alcohol), sex, gambling, food, or work - which they use to modulate their mood and self-esteem. They try to control their addiction and people around them in order to maintain the addiction. Meanwhile, they are controlled by it. Abstinence or sobriety allows them to work on the underlying issues of codependency. Recovery includes regaining autonomy and self-esteem, and the ability to manage their thinking, emotions and life problems.

Narcissists Are Codependent, Too
Writers often distinguish narcissists and codependents as opposites, but surprisingly, though their outward behavior may differ, they share many psychological traits. In fact, narcissists exhibit core codependent symptoms of shame, denial, control, dependency (unconscious), and dysfunctional communication and boundaries, all leading to intimacy problems. One study showed a significant correlation between narcissism and codependency. Although most narcissists can be classified as codependent, the reverse isn't true - most codependents aren't narcissists. They don't

exhibit common traits of exploitation, entitlement, and lack of empathy.

Dependency

Codependency is a disorder of a "lost self." Codependents have lost their connection to their innate self. Instead, their thinking and behavior revolve around a person, substance, or process. Narcissists also suffer from a lack of connection to their true self. In its place, they're identified with their ideal self. Their inner deprivation and lack of connection to their real self make them dependent on others for validation. Consequently, like other codependents, their self-image, thinking, and behavior is other-oriented in order to stabilize and validate their self-esteem and fragile ego.

Ironically, despite declared high self-regard, narcissists crave recognition from others and have an insatiable need to be admired - to get their "narcissistic supply." This makes them as dependent on recognition from others as an addict is on their addiction.

Shame

Shame is at the core of codependency and addiction. It stems from growing up in a dysfunctional family. Narcissists' inflated self-opinion is commonly mistaken for self-love. However, exaggerated self-flattery and arrogance merely assuage unconscious, internalized shame that is common among codependents.

Children develop different ways of coping with the anxiety, insecurity, and hostility that they experience growing up in dysfunctional families. Internalized shame can result despite parents' good intentions and lack of overt abuse. To feel safe, children adopt coping patterns that give rise to an ideal self. One strategy is to accommodate other people and seek their love, affection, and approval. Another is to seek recognition, mastery, and domination over others. Stereotypical codependents fall into the first category, and narcissists the second. They seek power and control of their environment in order to get their needs met. Their pursuit of prestige, superiority, and power help them to avoid feeling inferior, vulnerable, needy, and helpless at all costs.

These ideals are natural human needs; however, for codependents and narcissists, they're compulsive and thus neurotic. Additionally, the more a person pursues their ideal self, the further they depart from their real self, which only increases their insecurity, false self, and sense of shame.

Denial

Denial is a core symptom of codependency. Codependents are generally in denial of their codependency and often their feelings and many needs. Similarly, narcissists deny feelings, particularly those that express vulnerability. Many won't admit to feelings of inadequacy, even to themselves. They disown and often project onto others feelings that they consider "weak," such as longing, sadness, loneliness, powerlessness, guilt, fear, and variations of them. Anger makes them feel powerful. Rage, arrogance, envy, and contempt are defenses to underlying shame.

Codependents deny their needs, especially emotional needs, which were neglected or shamed growing up. Some codependents act self-sufficient and readily put others needs first. Other codependents are demanding of people to satisfy their needs. Narcissists also deny emotional needs. They won't admit that they're being demanding and needy because having needs makes them feel dependent and weak. They judge as needy.

Although narcissists don't usually put the needs of others first, some narcissists are actually people-pleasers and can be very generous. In addition to securing the attachment of those they depend on, often their motive is for recognition or to feel superior or grandiose by virtue of the fact that they're able to aid people they consider inferior. Like other codependents, they may feel exploited by and resentful toward the people they help.

Many narcissists hide behind a facade of self-sufficiency

and aloofness when it comes to needs for emotional closeness, support, grieving, nurturing, and intimacy. The quest of power protects them from experiencing the humiliation of feeling weak, sad, afraid, or wanting or needing anyone-ultimately, to avoid rejection and feeling shame. Only the threat of abandonment reveals how dependent they truly are.

Dysfunctional Boundaries

Like other codependents, narcissists have unhealthy boundaries, because theirs weren't respected growing up. They don't experience other people as separate but as extensions of themselves. As a result, they project thoughts and feelings onto others and blame them for their shortcomings and mistakes, all of which they cannot tolerate in themselves. Additionally, the lack of boundaries makes them thin-skinned, highly reactive, and defensive and causes them to take everything personally.

Most codependents share these patterns of blame, reactivity, defensiveness, and taking things personally. The behavior and degree or direction of feelings might vary, but the underlying process is similar. For example, many codependents react with self-criticism, self-blame, or withdrawal, while others react with aggression and criticism or blame of someone else. Yet, both behaviors are reactions to shame and demonstrate dysfunctional boundaries. (In some cases, confrontation or withdrawal might be an appropriate response, but not if it's a habitual, compulsive reaction.

Dysfunctional Communication

Like other codependents, narcissists' communication is dysfunctional. They generally lack assertiveness skills. Their communication often consists of criticism, demands, labeling, and other forms of verbal abuse. On the other hand, some narcissists intellectualize, obfuscate, and are indirect. Like other codependents, they find it difficult to identify and clearly state their feelings. Although they may express opinions and take positions more easily than other codependents, they

5.2 What is the Difference Between Codependency and Just Caring a lot About Someone?

codependency is the habit of avoiding oneself by focusing on another person. When one is having a codependent relationship, healthy love, respect and trust are compromised. If a codependent pattern has gone too far, establishing an important relationship on better footing may seem almost impossible.

Codependency is often a pattern that develops over time so it can be hard to see. It is also reinforced by occasional payoffs - both on the conscious and unconscious levels. Conscious payoffs may include feeling needed and useful. And you need not feel alone, even when you are because that other person is on your mind. Other conscious payoffs may include the experiences of infatuation or drama, which can give rise to feelings of romance or excitement that one might be afraid would otherwise pass them by.

Unconscious roots of codependency run deeper. Sometimes, people develop codependency as a life-long strategy of handling fear and trauma by focusing on others. In some families, about the only positive attention a child gets is when they are being useful and undemanding. As adults, these people often end up caretaking others beyond what is useful to either person. A person who is frequently criticized and judged at any age can become vulnerable to believing that they are not worthy of their own support and attention. These are just a few of co dependency's causes.

Ultimately, the worst thing about codependency is that it puts you in the backseat of your own life.

To be in the backseat of one's own life means that one's own natural talents and abilities may not be fully realized or even recognized. Because codependency is draining, codependent people may find that they do not have the energy or confidence they need to carry out personal goals, including finding the kind of love they deserve. The habit of focusing too much on others means that ultimately, a person will miss taking charge of the only thing anyone can really take charge of - their own life.

If you think you may have codependent leanings, you are not alone. If you feel stuck in codependent patterns with someone you care about, there is a silver lining: because codependency is a habitual state, it can be changed. Although this self-stifling pattern may not dissolve overnight, there are many tools available if you are serious about freeing yourself from it.

First, it is very important that you find supportive people that you can trust to help you break the codependency habit. To try to break this kind of habit just by reading about it is like trying to learn to swim without getting into the water. Find supportive friends and family with whom to talk. Also, it can be helpful to work with a therapist who understands codependency in order to develop a greater understanding of not only what you want to change but how you plan to get there. You may also want to attend group therapy, or try 12-step groups like Co-dependents Anonymous (CoDA) or Al-Anon. Groups like these can be motivating because you will find people there who are already working on issues similar to yours.

Here are some other tools to help you to free yourself of codependency:
•   Keep a journal. Write about what you are grateful for, what you want out of your life, and what is stopping you. Self-focus is easier when you can actually see your thoughts on paper.
•   Pleasing yourself has its own reward. Remember what activities or hobbies you like and do them - even if no one else in your life wants to do them with you.
•   Become more aware of your inner world. Take time

73

from your day to contemplate and meditate. If you remember your dreams at night, write them down.

• Take a relationship inventory. Who in your current life makes a better or a worse person out of you when you are with them? You don't have to be someone's friend just because they want you to be. Seek out people who help you to grow inwardly.

• Stop "enabling" others. If someone you are helping is not improving, check in with yourself. How do you feel - are you worried or resentful? Is your "help" really helping?

• Avoid the payoffs of codependency, such as approval for doing more than your share, or getting sucked into drama and infatuation. These are inner enemies. Note what feelings different people and places bring up for you.

• When you find you are obsessed, take time and space away from the person or thing you are obsessed with. Setting interpersonal boundaries can help to put your focus back on yourself. Generally, others will respect you more for it as well.

• Develop a sense of spirituality. This can be as simple as appreciating nature, focusing on a hobby or talking to a wise person. Developing a concept of having a higher power within yourself that has answers for you is also helpful.

The most important tool in all of this is that you think well of yourself. This may feel awkward or even like you are just pretending at first. Yet it is critically important to making progress. One of the most heartbreaking things is to watch a codependent person trying so hard to fix things, only to fail and then turn on themselves. People can treat themselves much more harshly than anyone else would. Codependency and low-self esteem go hand in hand so let go of that inner voice that says you can't change. The beginning of recovery can be just as simple as allowing oneself to begin to see what is good and true about oneself.

It is my hope that you will start to rid yourself of codependent patterns with those you care about by trying out at least one of these tools today. To do so is to begin the process of learning what you need to know about healing your life and your relationships - from the inside out.

frequently have trouble listening and are dogmatic and inflexible. These are signs of dysfunctional communication that evidence insecurity and lack of respect for the other person.

Control

Like other codependents, narcissists seek to control. Control over our environment helps us to feel safe. The greater our anxiety and insecurity, the greater is our need for control. When we're dependent on others for our security, happiness, and self-worth, what people think, say, and do become paramount to our sense of well-being and even safety. We'll try to control them directly or indirectly with people-pleasing, lies, or manipulation. If we're frightened or ashamed of our feelings, such as anger or grief, then we attempt to control our feelings. Other people's anger or grief will upset us, so that they must be avoided or controlled, too.

Intimacy

Finally, the combination of all these patterns makes intimacy challenging for narcissists and codependents, alike. Relationships can't thrive without clear boundaries that afford partners freedom and respect. They require that we're autonomous, have assertive communication skills, and self-esteem.

CHAPTER 6

CODEPENDENCY AND THE BRAIN

Codependency is both additive and breeds addictions. People's actions are usually motivated by rewards and, in this case, the reward is the temporary disconnection from their painful pasts by focusing on others and the belief that doing so will bring them happiness and fulfillment, as they attempt to avoid their own emptiness and negative self-feelings.

Although they feel flawed because of their upbringing, the real flaw is that an external source can fill and replace an internal one. The more they look toward others, the more they deny and disconnect from their own needs, wants, and deficits.

"This love deficit condemns us to an existence of addiction, para-alcoholism, codependence, or seeking some other outward source to heal an inward feeling of being unwanted or defective," according to the "Adult Children of Alcoholics" textbook (World Service Organization, 2006, p. 438).

Although certain strategies can temporarily relieve their adverse condition, such as avoiding, depending, obsessing, and compulsive, excessive reliance upon them, as ultimately occurs with codependence, exaggerates them and elevates them to addiction levels, transforming their "benefits" into deficits. Yet doing so is not a solution, since it fails to address the underlying reason for it and only ends up creating what can be considered a byproduct problem.

The more a person seeks gratification to rise above his unresolved past, the more he reinforces the neuro-pathway to pleasure in his brain, cementing the belief that this "other-person" addiction can provide satisfaction through external means so much so, in fact, that the moment his "fix" is removed or is even threatened to be removed, he crashes and falls back into his pit of pain.

Like all addictions, however, it effects to not end there: indeed, the brain eventually creates a tolerance for them, demanding ever greater quantities, frequencies, and intensities to satisfy him, until he becomes that proverbial binary star, orbiting around others, unable to function without them, as he becomes nothing more than his mirror image.

"Just as we develop a tolerance to the effects of chemicals, we develop a tolerance to the effects of our behaviors... ," according to Sharon Wegscheider-Cruse and Joseph Cruse in their book, "Understanding Codependency: The Science Behind it and How to Break the Cycle" (Health Communications, 2012, p. 33). "This vicious, one-way circle is a trap that ends in depression, isolation, institutions, and sometimes death."

Excessive psychological and emotional reliance on others is, in essence, an exaggeration of normal personality traits and can ultimately disable a person, culminating in the disease of codependence. The way the body can quickly become dependent upon mood-altering chemicals, it can equally become physically dependent upon behaviors to the point that compulsions serve as his armament.

"The disease of codependency can be seen as a personal struggle with a variety of compulsive disorders," Wegscheider-Cruse and Cruse wrote (Ibid, p. 131). "People... have lived in a condition of denial, distorted feelings, and compulsive behaviors, and as a result, they have developed low self-worth, deep shame, inadequacy, and anger."

But the codependent erroneously believes two mistruths. One is that he is intrinsically flawed and the other is that someone outside of himself can fill what he already possesses inside of himself.

Origins, Definitions, and Manifestations of the Disease

The codependent seed is planted when a person turns his responsibility for his life and happiness to either his ego (false self) or others, becoming preoccupied with them to the extent that he temporarily rises above his own pain and, in its extreme, can entirely forget who he even is, when he consistently mirrors someone else-in other words, if he looks out here to the other, he will not have to look in there to himself.

"Codependence, (a major manifestation of the adult child syndrome), is a disease of lost self-hood," according to Dr. Charles L. Whitfield in his book, "Co-Dependence: Healing the Human Condition" (Health Communications, 1991, p. 3). "It can mimic, be associated with, aggravate, and even lead to many of the physical, mental, emotional, or spiritual conditions that befall us in daily life.

"When we focus outside of ourselves, we lose touch with what is inside of us: beliefs, thoughts, feelings, decisions, choices, experiences, wants, needs, sensations, intuitions... These and more are part of an exquisite feedback system that we can call our inner life."

In short, a person can sever his connection with his consciousness and consciousness is who he really is.

Like expecting a home appliance to operate without plugging it into an electric socket, a codependent may merge with and feed off of another to such an extent that he no longer believes he can function independently.

The origins of the malady are the same as those which cause the adult child syndrome.

"The hallmark of codependency is taking care of people who should have been taking care of you," according to Dr.

Susan Powers of the Caron Treatment Centers.

Instead of being self-centered and expecting to get their needs met, children from dysfunctional, alcoholic, or abusive homes are forced, at a very early age, to become other- or parent-centered, meeting their needs, attempting to resolve or fix their deficiencies, and sometimes making Herculean efforts to achieve their love in what may be considered an ultimate role reversal. If this dynamic could be verbally expressed, the parent would say, "What I can't do, you're expected to do yourself, substituting you for me."

And this reality may well extend beyond themselves, since they are often forced to replace their parents during times that their younger siblings have the need for them, becoming surrogate mothers and fathers. In essence, they disregard their own need for a parent and become one themselves. Instead of being nurtured, they cultivate codependence, since it places them on a path that will entail seeking it in others.

"Our experience shows that the codependent rupture, which creates an outward focus to gain love and affection, is created by a dysfunctional childhood," according to the "Adult Children of Alcoholics" textbook (World Service Organization, "The soul rupture is the abandonment by our parents or caregivers (and) sets us up for a life of looking outward for love and safety that never comes."

This condition is only exacerbated by the same parents who neither support nor permit a child to express or heal his hurts-and may actually be met with denial or shame if he tries to do so-leaving him little choice but to stuff and swallow them, resulting in a repressed, but the mounting accumulation of unresolved negative emotions. After repeated squelching of a child's observations, feelings, and reactions, in essence, his reality-he progressively disconnects from his true self and denies his crucial inner cues.

Unraveling, he is poised on the threshold that leads from into out-that is, toward others and away from himself, sparking the conflict between his once true and since replaced false self, which manifests itself as codependence.

Forced, additionally, to focus on his parent's moods, attitudes, and behaviors further plant the roots of this condition but nevertheless becomes a necessary survival tactic for two primary reasons.

First and foremost, children assume responsibility for their parents' deficiencies and ill-treatment by justifying it, erroneously reasoning that their own flaws, lack of worth, and general unlovability are the culprits for the withholds of their validation and acceptance, thus shifting the burden from the ones who should be carrying it to the one who should not.

Secondly, adopting a sixth sense concerning their parents' moods becomes a safety gauge and enables them to emotionally and physiologically prepare themselves for what has most likely become habitual and even cyclical negative confrontations of verbal and physical abuse.

As episodes of "expected abnormalcy," they add insurmountable layers of trauma to the original but no longer remembered one. Unable, then or now, to use the body's fight or flight survival mechanisms, yet still drowned in a flood of stress hormones (cortisol) and elevated energy, they have no choice but to tuck themselves into the inner child protective sanctuary they created at a very young age as the only realizable "solution" to the parental-threatened and -inflicted danger, enduring, tolerating, and downright surviving the unfair power play and "punishment" they may believe is being administered because of "deserved discipline."

Like signals, a mere frown on or cringe of a parent's face may prime the child for the episodes he knows will assuredly follow. So thick can the tension in the air become at these times, that he can probably cut it with a knife.

Part of the wounding, which reduces a person's sense of self and esteem and increases his feeling of emptiness, occurs as a result of projective identification. Volatility charged, yet unable to get to the center of or bore through his emotional pain, a parent may project, like a movie on to a screen, parts of himself on to another, such as his vulnerable, captive child, until that child takes on and identifies with the projection.

Releasing and relieving himself, the sender, (the parent) does not have to own or even take responsibility for his negative feelings. If the recipient (the child) ultimately acts them out after repeated projected implanting, whose emotions now mount into uncontainable proportions, the sender may berate or belittle him for them, in an ultimate out-of-persona dynamic, which transfers emotions from one to the other.

"If we have unhealthy boundaries, we are like sponges that absorb the painful, conflicted material of others sent from their inner life," wrote Whitfield in "Co-Dependence: Healing the Human Condition". "It is clearly not ours, yet we soak it up.

"(This only causes) the true self to go into hiding to protect itself from the overwhelming pain of mistreatment, abuse, lack of being affirmed and mirrored in a healthy way, and the double and other negative messages from toxic others around it," he noted.

These incidents, needless to say, become breeding grounds for both the adult child syndrome and its codependent manifestation.

"The adult child syndrome is somewhat interchangeable with the diagnosis of codependence," according to the "Adult Children of Alcoholics" textbook (World Service Organization). "There are many definitions for codependence; however, the general consensus is that codependent people tend to focus on the wants and needs of others rather than their own. By doing so, the codependent or adult child can avoid his or her own feelings of low self-worth. A codependent focuses on others and their problems to such an extent that the codependent's life is often adversely affected."

Part of a codependent's breeding occurs because a child needs his parents for his emotional and psychological development, yet he often dips into a dry well when he connects with them to achieve this goal, emerging dissatisfied, unfulfilled, and almost stung by the negative, rejecting energy. He may, in fact, implement several strategies to attain what he vitally needs, but will often fail, since his parents themselves never received what he seeks because of their own dysfunctional or incomplete childhoods.

If they could be considered profit-and-loss statements, they would most likely show an emotional deficit and, eventually, so, too, will the child, prompting his ultimate outward- and other- focus.

Bombarded with parental blame and shame, a child can quickly believe that he causes others' negative or detrimental actions by virtue of his sheer existence as if he were a negatively influencing entity and may carry both this belief and its burden for most of his life.

"As children, we took responsibility for our parents' anger, rage, blame, or pitifulness." according to the "Adult Children of Alcoholics" textbook (World Service Organization, 2006, p. 7). "This mistaken perception, born in childhood, is the root of our codependent behavior as adults."

Dr. Charles L. Whitfield uncovers an even deeper cause.

"The cause of codependence is a wounding of the true self to such an extent that, to survive, it had to go into hiding most of the time, with the subsequent running of its life by the false or codependent self," he wrote in "Co-Dependence: Healing the Human Condition" (Health Communications). "It is thus a disease of lost self-hood."

"The child's vulnerable true self is wounded so often that to protect (it), it defensively submerges (splits off) deep within the unconscious part of the psyche," he also noted.

This split, one of the many detriments of codependence, arrests this development, as his inner child remains mired in the initial trauma that necessitated its creation. Although his chronological age may advance, his emotional and psychological progress remains suspended, creating the adult child. His body and the physical statue may suggest the first part of this "adult" designation to others, but his reactions may more closely approximate the second "child" part of it.

Conflicted, he may engage in an internal battle he does not entirely understand, as his adult side wishes and needs to function at an age-appropriate level, but his child half clings to the sting of his unresolved harm, seeking sanctuary and safety. He is unable to satisfy both.

People naturally seek relief from pain and addictions and compulsions, a second manifestation of codependence, is one of the methods they employ, especially since they lack any understanding about their affliction. Because they spark the brain's reward system, however, they only provide temporary, fleeting fixes, not solutions.

Exacerbating this dilemma is the fact that they flow from a false sense of self, which itself can only be mollified, quelled, or deceptively filled by these means.

Since their childhood circumstances were both familiar and normal to them, they subconsciously may also attract, now as adult children, those with similar upbringings by means of sixth-sense intuitions or identifications, creating a third codependent manifestation.

"On (an even) deeper level," according to Whitefield in "Co-Dependence: Healing the Human Condition" (Health Communications), "they may also be drawn to one another in a search to heal their unfinished business and, perhaps more importantly, their lost self."

Nevertheless, inter-relating with others who themselves

function from the deficit-dug holes in their souls, they only re-create the childhood dynamics they experienced with their parents, substituting their partners for them and suffering a secondary form of wounding over and above the primary one sustained in childhood. In effect, they become another link in the intergenerational chain.

Even if they encounter whole, loving people, who are able to provide the needed acceptance and validation they crave, they are unable to accept it, since they do not function from the true self that otherwise could-nor, in the event, do they even believe that they deserve it. It bounces off of them like an image on a mirror, only creating yet a fourth byproduct of codependence.

Aside from the codependent foundation laid in childhood by dysfunctional parents, who themselves were wounded and caused the adult child syndrome upon which its codependent aspect was based, the condition is far more prevalent in society than may at first be apparent. Continually, but sometimes subtly modeled, it can almost be considered contagious.

Identifying Codependence

One of the frustrating aspects of codependence is that it either wears a disguise or remains altogether hidden, prompting the behavioral modifications and almost-scripted roles of those who suffer from it, such as rescuer, people-pleaser, perfectionist, overachiever, victim, martyr, lost child, comedian, mascot, bully, and even abuser, that deludes others to the fact that it is present. The motivation for such behavior is not always immediately apparent.

Nevertheless, there are several traits which characterize codependence.

Sparked by the need to protect the traumatized inner child and arising, in part, from disordered relationships, it results, first and foremost, in the creation of the false self, which replaces the genuine, intrinsic one, and becomes the root of all other addictions and compulsions. The emptier a person feels inside, the more he seeks to fill that void outside.

"Codependence is not only the most common addiction," according to Whitefield in "Co-Dependence: Healing the Human Condition" (Health Communications, 1991, pp. 5-6), "it is the base out of which all our other addictions and compulsions emerge. Underneath nearly every addiction and compulsion lies codependence. And what runs them is twofold: a sense of shame that our true self is somehow defective or inadequate, combined with the innate and healthy drive of our true self that does not realize and (cannot) express itself. The addiction, compulsion, or disorder becomes the manifestation of the erroneous notion that something outside ourselves can make us happy and fulfilled."

And underlying codependence is shame and a deep belief that the person is inadequate, incomplete, and flawed.

Avoiding his own negative feelings and painful past, he becomes externally and other-focused, yet is unable to genuinely connect with them, with himself, or with a Higher Power of his understanding through the false or pseudo-self, he was forced to create. In fact, this has the opposite or repelling effect.

His boundaries, another aspect of the disease, may be distorted, undefined, and extend beyond himself.

Finally, as a defense, codependence is learned, acquired, progressive, and inextricably tied to the adult child syndrome, since the false self serves as the link between the two.

Recovering from Codependency

Treatment for codependency often involves the exploration of early childhood issues and their connection to current dysfunctional behavior patterns. Getting in touch with deep-rooted feelings of hurt, loss, and anger will allow you to reconstruct appropriate relationship dynamics.

Psychotherapy is highly recommended as these personality characteristics are ingrained and difficult to change on your own. Choosing the right therapist can make all the difference in your recovery. You'll know you're on track when the following traits become part of your personality:

You nurture your own wants and desires and develop a connection to your inner world. You see yourself as self-reliant, smart, and capable.

You say goodbye to abusive behavior. Awareness, change, and growth is necessary for you and for your partner to overcome unhealthy relationship habits. Caretaking and enabling behavior is acknowledged and stopped.

You respond rather than react to your partner—and to others. Setting clear, firm boundaries means that you don't automatically react to everyone's thoughts and feelings. You tolerate other people's opinions and do not become defensive when you disagree. You recognize that your reaction is your responsibility. You adopt a healthy skepticism regarding what others say about you (good or bad), and your self-esteem doesn't rise and fall as a result. You say no, and you accept hearing no.

When you've recovered from codependency, you no longer feel compelled to stay in an unhealthy, painful relationship. You know that you are not responsible for anyone's happiness except for your own, and you can feel comfortable with the decision to walk away.

CHAPTER 7

HOW TO RECOVER FROM CODEPENDENCY

Recovery from codependency begins with developing self-esteem, self-acceptance, and self-love. It's a journey of self-reclamation – a discovery of who you really are beneath learned, false ideas. You gain the ability to express yourself assertively, pursue your passions, and prevent others from abusing you. Recovery also includes having fun, being kind and gentle with yourself, and for many people, developing their spiritual side. Changing codependent habits is impossible to do alone without the support of others and a guide to show the way. Read all you can and attend a 12-Step Program or seek psychotherapy.

Codependency is learned - learned inaccurate information that you're in some way not enough, that you don't matter, that your feelings are wrong, or that you don't deserve respect. These are the false beliefs that most codependents grow up with. They may not have been told these things directly, but have inferred it from behavior and attitudes of family and friends and events. Often these beliefs get handed down for generations. Changing them isn't easy and is difficult to do on your own, because it's hard to see others, let alone yourself, through a lens that's different than the one you grew up with.

Usually, people aren't conscious of these beliefs about themselves. The 19th Century neurologist Jean-Martin Charcot, the father of hypnosis, wrote that if there were a conflict between the will and the unconscious, the unconscious would always prevail. This explains what drives codependents' behavior and why we often fail to carry out our best intentions or act upon what we know is right. Charcot had a great influence on Freud, who studied with him.

Codependents have many fears and anxieties based upon false ideas about themselves and others. For example, many think that making a mistake is unacceptable and shameful. They become anxious about taking risks, trying something new, or expressing their opinion, because they're afraid of failure or looking foolish. Most don't realize that they unconsciously believe that they're unlovable, unlikable, flawed or somehow inadequate. Even if they're aware of these false beliefs, they're convinced of their truth. As a result, they're anxious about revealing who they are, and please, control, or impress others so that they'll be loved and not rejected. Still, other codependents withdraw from people, rather than risk abandonment. People judge themselves based upon their erroneous beliefs and imagine others are judging them, too.

The false belief about unworthiness undermines codependents' self-esteem and security and has serious consequences in their lives. They lack confidence and self-trust, live in doubt, and continually second-guess themselves. Many don't feel worthy of being in a position of authority or having success, or even happiness. Those who are convinced that they're bad can end up in relationships with people who are emotionally or physically abusive, which reinforces and worsens their low self-esteem. At a conscious level, they may be indignant and think that they deserve better, but still, they stay and try to get the abuser to approve of them. Some stay because they believe the abuser "loves" them, which helps them overcome the belief that they're unlovable or that no one else will.

Similarly, many codependents have repeated relationships with men or women who are emotionally, or even physically, unavailable. They don't feel that they deserve to be loved on a consistent basis. The unconscious belief is that "I have to win someone's love for it to mean anything." There may be opportunities for a relationship with someone loving and available, but they're not interested. Instead, they're excited about someone whose love they have to earn. They have to win it for it to count.

When you grow up with the message that you shouldn't feel a certain way or it's unsafe to express certain feelings, you start to believe it. An example is being told not to get too excited, being punished for anger, having your distress or sadness ignored. Some shaming parents will tell their child not to cry, "or I'll give you something to cry about." As adults, codependents judge and dishonor their feelings. They hide them - sometimes even from themselves after years of suppression. If they don't believe that it's all right, "Christian," or "spiritual" to feel angry, they may behave passive-aggressively, become depressed, or have physical symptoms, unaware of how angry they are. This is destructive to relationships. Some people withhold sex or have affairs because they're angry, instead of talking about the relationship problems.

Codependents also don't believe they have rights or that their needs matter, especially emotional needs, such as for appreciation, support, kindness, being understood, and loved. Most will put others' needs ahead of their own, don't say "no" because they're afraid others will criticize or leave them, triggering their underlying belief in being inadequate and unlovable. They often give or do more in relationships or at work for this reason. Self-sacrifice causes codependents to feel unappreciated and resentful. They wonder why they're unhappy, never thinking it's because they're not getting their needs met. Moreover, because often they're not aware of their needs, they don't take steps to have them met. If they do know, they can't ask for what they want. It would feel humiliating. Instead, they don't take steps to meet their needs and expect others to do so - without disclosing them! These hidden expectations contribute to conflict in relationships.

Changing beliefs starts with awareness.
•   You can become aware of your beliefs by paying attention to the way you talk to yourself.
•   Write down all the negative things you say to yourself.
•   Note the gap between your intentions and actions.
•   Journal about this discrepancy and your interactions with others.
•   Analyze your beliefs motivating your behavior. Ask yourself where your beliefs came from.

4 Tips for Recovery from Codependence
1.   Physically Take Care of Yourself
The first 90 days of recovery are the most important times during the healing process. This is the period when most people relapse and turn back to the old ways that landed them in rehab in the first place.

It's critical, then, that you keep your body in good health throughout the process by eating healthy foods so you'll feel as energetic and strong as possible. Not only will you be giving your body the nutrition it needs to recover from your substance use disorder, but your mental health will also experience a boost as well thanks to all those extra vitamins and minerals.

What's more, getting extra exercise will help keep your mind off of the addiction while relieving stress at the same time.

2. Manage Your Stress

Stress is one of the key risk factors for relapsing, both into destructive personal habits as well as destructive patterns of substance abuse. It may be difficult to do so (especially if you're coming out of a codependent relationship) but try to keep your stress levels down while you adjust to a life outside of codependence.

When you find yourself becoming especially stressed out, try to practice some calming breathing exercises or looking at the problem objectively rather than emotionally. Keeping a cool head is critical to maintaining the healthy lifestyle habits you learned about during rehab and is essential if you want to avoid falling back into old habits.

3. Stop Trying to Control Everything

An incessant need to control is one of the core codependent behaviors that you need to get over before living a healthy, interdependent life. And while it's essential to let go every now and then, doing so is easier said than done.

A great way to start embracing whatever life throws at you rather than trying to control every aspect of your life is by trying new things. Head to a different restaurant that you've never tried before. Try taking up new hobbies like painting, karaoke, or exercising.

The important part is getting outside of your element (just a bit) to help you realize that the world won't end if you give up a little control.

4. Stick to Your Guns

Last but certainly not least, live up to your new standards no matter what. You've struggled to regain your self-confidence and kick your substance abuse problem. You've certainly suffered your fair share of emotional turmoil and physical pain. As such, you must do everything in your power to prevent relapsing into old habits.

If you've separated yourself from your codependent partner, that means keeping your contact with them extremely limited if they even need to be seen at all. Like substance abuse, codependency can come back full swing from just a single trigger. Knowing how to cope with those triggers (or avoid them entirely) is crucial to your recovery.

If you're working on fixing your codependent relationship, preventing relapse means enforcing the new boundaries that you've set. Don't make excuses for your partner and certainly don't avoid bringing it up when they've violated those boundaries either. Reinventing your take on relationships can certainly be hard. But it's only worth doing if you can actually stick to it.

Tips on Overcoming Codependent Behavior

After you've taken the first step towards recovery, the next step is to start eliminating your codependent behaviors. It may be difficult at first but it's important to remember that your behaviors are contributing to a toxic and unhealthy association that simply needs to stop.

Here are a few tips to get you started towards interdependence:

1. First thing's first, get treatment for your (or your partner's) substance abuse problem.

Nothing is going to change if your relationship is still fueled by unclear thinking, emotional volatility, and physical addiction. And even if it does temporarily, that respite from the abuse that it causes will most likely be short-lived.

2. Start putting an emphasis on communicating your feelings.

The #1 reason couples split up is a lack of communication. Funny enough, one of the biggest contributors to the development of a codependent relationship is also a lack of communication.

You may be used to ignoring your feelings or even not fully understanding what they are and where they're coming from. But the more you start to express your feelings, the better you'll get at identifying what's actually wrong and communicating what you want to change. Having a voice is having power

3.   Learn to process your childhood

Codependency has a profound link to past trauma during childhood. As a child, you may have been abandoned by a parent, forgotten by a friend, or ignored and made to feel useless by someone you loved and respected. In order to overcome your codependent habits, it's essential that you actively begin to acknowledge these feelings so you can overcome them.

Next time you feel an overwhelming sense of fear or anxiety, try to think back to times when you were younger that you felt the same emotion. Pick out specific details about the situation and really take a look at why you were experiencing that feeling in the first place. And most importantly, recognize that in most cases, what happened to you was not actually your fault.

This simple acknowledgment can have a cascading effect that helps you understand that the emotions and compulsions causing your codependent behavior today don't need to rule your life.

4.   Treat Addiction First.

If your spouse or family member is struggling with addiction, determine if they're also dealing with symptoms of a co-occurring disorder like post-traumatic stress disorder before seeking out a treatment center. While you may think that it's better to treat the addiction first and the other mood disorder later, the truth is that these two mental health issues actually tend to exacerbate each other. As such, treating them one at a time may never work since they're both constantly adding fuel to each other's flame.

Instead, take the time to find a dual-diagnosis addiction facility that's equipped to treat both disorders at the same time. Doing so will ensure your loved one's rehabilitation is far more successful and the likelihood of eliminating codependency will be even higher.

5. Recognize Denial

The second step to healing is to really be frank with yourself and recognize the problem. There probably a very good chance you have intellectualized and justified your codependence over time. While it can feel scary to admit to being codependent and/or involved in a dysfunctional relationship, honesty with yourself is really the first step toward healing.

6. Look to Your Past

The first step on your path to rescue is to take a look at your own past to reveal and understand experiences that may have contributed to your codependency. What is your family history? Is there emotional neglect and abuse? Were there events that led to you distancing yourself from your true inner emotions and ignoring your own needs?

This can be a difficult process and one that involves thinking about and re-experiencing childhood emotions. You may even find that you feel angry, sad, shameful or guilty as you think about this.

Note: This type of exploration can be very emotional and stressful and is often best done in a safe therapy relationship.

7. Detach and Disentangle Yourself

In order to truly work on and improve ourselves, we have to first disconnect from the things we are troubled with. Personal growth will require giving up our preoccupation and over-involvement with trying to control, rescue, or change others and our defaulting to always trying to please someone else.

This means taking a deep breath, letting go and acknowledging we cannot fix problems that are not necessarily ours to fix. What problems do we "own" and what problems are "owned" by others in our lives? It's about really trying to differentiate where you end and others begin.

8. Practice Self-care

Giving up your attempts to constantly please others is a good start to healing, but learning self-care is absolutely necessary as well. It's super important that you really begin to explore and become aware of your own thoughts, feelings, and needs. We also need to learn how to communicate them to others in our relationships. This may feel very hard and even foreign to us at first as if you are being especially self-centered. But that's part of learning how to take care of our own needs.

Self-care means taking care of ourselves physically — eating healthy, getting enough sleep, exercising regularly, and going to our doctor and taking any prescribed medications. Self-care also means caring for ourselves emotionally, making social connections, finding happy positive activities to fill our time, and allowing ourselves emotional downtime and rest if we need it. It also means really getting in touch and examining our own thoughts, opinions, values, wants and needs — regardless of what other's opinions are. Good strategies to do this can be writing and reflecting through the process of journaling and of course, going to therapy.

9. Learn to Say No!

One of the best ways you can begin to set healthy boundaries is to learn to say no to situations that are damaging to your own well-being. This will feel uncomfortable at first, but the more you do it, the easier it will become. We have the right to say no to others and often we don't need to give them a long explanation. We have the right to say no to things that are not the best for us. This is not about being selfish and uncaring towards others — but it's about setting boundaries and putting our own needs first.

10. Be Kinder to Yourself!

Be kind to yourself! This is about self-compassion and treating yourself the same way you would treat the others you love!

7.2   Setting Boundaries to End Codependency

One of the most important steps in breaking outside of your own codependency is to set boundaries within your relationship. As a caretaker, it might be especially difficult in any situation to say no to your loved one.

But doing so is undoubtedly the only way you will ever be able to salvage the relationship and transform it into one that's both healthy and respectful.

Here are a few tips to help you start setting reasonable boundaries for your loved one:

•   Don't set boundaries when either you or your partner are in any way under the influence, whether by substances or by intense emotions. Presenting boundaries with a clear head will help you stay calm and collected and reduce the chances of things spiraling out of control.

•   Communicate your boundaries unabashedly. This one can be tough since you've probably been conditioned to feel ashamed when talking about your own needs. But if you can put on a stoic face (even if it is just a mask at first) it'll help your partner take you more seriously.

•   Be specific. Communicate the exact actions you want to stop or changes you want to see as well as what you're prepared to do if these requests aren't met. They should be within reason, of course, but don't be afraid to threaten to leave the relationship as long as you're prepared to do so.

•   And finally, communicate why you are doing what you're doing. Tell them about how their actions have made you feel in the past and why you deserve a change in the future. Specificity here is crucial.

CHAPTER 8

RAISING A CODEPENDENT CHILD

In the past codependency was associated with the person who enabled an alcoholic or drug addict. These days codependency has become associated with emotional dependencies in a relationship. All relationships involve a dependency on another person to some extent. However, when an individual compromises their own values and wants to avoid rejection and anger they are exhibiting codependent behaviors.

The reason why this is so important for parents to understand is that its origins start in childhood. So if you are doing the following three things you may be planting the seeds of codependency.

1. Being inflexible (or the type A "super parent")

If you are the type of person who has a rigid plan of how and when things are done you do not allow your child an opportunity to voice their choice. If you are so in control of their schedule, their food choices, their clothing choices, or their playmates you are restricting your child from having the opportunity to explore their choices. You send out a message loud and clear to your child that they are not responsible for their choices or decisions and someone else has all the power. As they grow older they are likely to seek out relationships in which someone else has all the power and

97

control.

What can you do? Allow your child some freedom of choice. If it is not a safety issue then it is negotiable. Let go of the need to be in control and allow your child the freedom to grow and learn, even from their mistakes!

2. Having your child meet your needs

many parents who fall into this trap but do not see that they are doing this. If you are not fulfilling yourself in other areas of your life, like your relationships, your work, or your passions, you may default to living vicariously through your child. When you spend more energy on your child's interests and less on what gives your life meaning and pleasure you model codependent self-sacrificing behaviors. You also unconsciously teach your child that their value comes from pleasing you. The cute "look mom" behavior phase that most kids go through when they want your approval may continue into adulthood.

What can you do? Get your own needs met with positive relationships and ways to replenish yourself. Instead of constant praise ask your child how they thought they did. Encourage them to self-praise.

3. Wanting to solve problems for them

When they come home and talk about a mean peer or a problem at school what do you do? Do you react and rescue, slipping into your parent problem-solver mode and coming up with a plan of action? Essentially you are taking control of their ability to solve the problems they are encountering. This sends your child the message that they are not competent or responsible enough to figure out how to solve their problems and that someone else needs to do it for them. Imagine what this will look like as they become adults? Will they choose relationships where another person will tell them what to do?

What can you do? Safety first, everything else is negotiable! If it is not a physical or psychological safety issue allow your child the opportunity to figure out how to solve the problem. If you LISTEN, without offering advice, your child will likely figure out some things they can do differently.

The reason why so many children have success in our programs is that we offer a safe place for them to explore their thoughts, feelings, and choices. When given an opportunity, children will come up with creative ways to solve their problems. As adults, we can offer support and encouragement as they explore their choices.

One last important thing. If you find that you are doing one or more of the behaviors above, congratulations! That's right, Congratulations! Why? Because it means that you are aware of what you are doing, and awareness is the first step in making changes. So the next time you notice you are defaulting to one of the behaviors above, STOP, and explore what other things you can do.

8.2   Types of Abuse that Contribute to Codependency

The child may have experienced sexual, emotional or physical abuse in the dysfunctional family. In addition, there may have been a family member who suffered from chronic physical or mental ailment. Another causative scenario is a family member who was attached to addictions such as gambling, binge eating, workaholism, romantic fantasy, pornography, sex, alcohol or drugs. The child grows up thinking they should serve or protect the abused or suffering family member. Slowly, they also become as sick as the one they are protecting or helping.

CHAPTER 9

CODEPENDENT OR SIMPLY DEPENDENT: WHAT'S THE BIG DIFFERENCE?

Being codependent is hardly the same thing as simply being dependent. And in some ways, it's crucial that these two types of dependency be recognized as distinct (as too often hasn't been the case). Not that codependent individuals aren't dependent on others. But, paradoxically, they're primarily dependent on the other person's dependence on them. So what's the peculiar dynamic operating in such relationships? For—as this post will illustrate—it's not very healthy for either party.

It's also important to distinguish codependent relationships from interdependent ones. For as defined psychologically, codependence is clearly maladaptive and dysfunctional. It may have a certain mutuality to it, but it's negatively symbiotic in a way interdependency is not. Having dependency needs isn't by itself unhealthy. We all have them. In an interdependent relationship, however, each party is able to comfortably rely on the other for help, understanding, and support. It's a "value added" kind of thing. The relationship contributes to both individuals' resilience, resourcefulness,

100

and inner strength. All the same, each party remains self-sufficient and self-determining. They maintain a clear identity apart from the relationship and are quite able to stand on their own two feet.

On the contrary, a codependent union is one where both parties are over-dependent on each other. It's a relationship in which the two individuals lean so heavily on one another that both of them are left "off-balance." In their desperately trying to get core dependency needs to be met, their true identities are distorted, and their development and potential—personally, socially, and professionally—is stifled. The relationship is reciprocal only in that it enables both of them to avoid confronting their worst fears and self-doubts. As opposed to healthy dependency (defined here as interdependence), the codependent individual in such a relationship needs to be needed if they're to feel okay about themselves. They simply can't feel this way unless they're giving themselves up, or "sacrificing," themselves, for their partner. Sadly, without being depended upon (sometimes, virtually as a lifeline), they feel alone, inadequate, insecure, and unworthy.

Let's now delve deeper into the anxieties—and secret shame—of those who suffer from this malaise.

Generally, as children, the codependent's needy parents repeatedly gave them the message that their own wants and needs should be regarded as secondary to their caretakers'. To the extent that these children neglected their needs and focused on their parents', they could feel valued. But to the degree that they allowed themselves to assert their own, quite legitimate, dependency needs, they were subject either to indirect punishment (say, the silent treatment) or direct (being verbally or physically attacked).

In so many words, they were told that they were selfish and should feel guilty about thinking only of themselves. And it should be noted here that in such families at least one of the parents was probably an addict, arrested in their development and (childishly) seeking to compensate for their own earlier deprivation through a "substitute" dependency on their child. That is, they defined the child's role in terms of serving them, not the reverse.

Most codependents, then, learned as children that to be "good enough" to be accepted by their parents they had to deny or repress many of their thoughts, feelings, and impulses. In attempting to secure their tenuous (and so anxiety-laden) parental bond, they were required to forget about what they really liked, wanted, and needed—even who they were. So it's only to be expected that once grown up and endeavoring to live a life of their own, they'd be saddled with a deep, internalized "program" regularly reminding them that to be accepted by others they had to make their own needs—which at this point they may only dimly recognize—subordinate to others'. Early emotional survival programs, once adaptive but no longer appropriate, continue to control their thoughts and actions.

So, as adults, how might they be characterized?

1.   Their self-esteem depends on the validation of others (i.e., they can't self-validate or, independently, approve of themselves).

2.   Their (fragile) sense of self-worth and well-being is extremely vulnerable, making them highly sensitive and reactive to others.

3.   Their ability to assert their needs in a relationship (and, assuming they're in a committed one, not just with their partner but with others as well) is highly constrained. And if they do assert them, they're likely to feel guilty afterward.

4.   Their sense of responsibility centers more on the other person's feelings, needs, wants, and desires than on their own. Consequently, others' attitudes, actions, and reactions typically govern what they say and do.

5.   Their basic ability to set boundaries with others— and possibly others' requests of, or demands on them—is highly restricted (as it was originally with their intrusive parents, who regularly "used" them to compensate for the

nurturing they themselves never received from their caretakers).

6.　　Their behavior is largely dictated by an underlying fear of being alone, and so feeling abandoned, spurned, or rejected.

7.　　Their feelings are experienced as less their own than tied to another's behavior.

8.　　Their sense of themselves in situations of discord is that they're victims, unable to be heard, sympathized with, or understood.

9.　　Their (compulsive?) loyalty to others can go substantially beyond what's warranted and may end up hurting them.

10.　　Their personal values are second-guessed, sacrificed, or ignored when they conflict with another's. To protect a relationship, they're actually ready to forfeit their own integrity.

Yet codependents—and this is one of the most fascinating aspects of their character—may not, outwardly, look dependent. That is, they can disguise, even beyond recognition, their urgent reliance on others to confirm their fundamental worth. How? By saying and doing things that make them seem quite in command, even controlling. Having learned in childhood to please and placate their parents, most of them can be "managerial" with others, and in ways that convey a contrary message about themselves.

To hide from others—and, indeed, from themselves as well—that their lives really feel out of control, they can:

• Become the person that others depend on, making them look stronger, mentally and emotionally, than they really are. In fact, it's precisely because they believe they can't, or shouldn't, depend on others (again, consider their self-absorbed caretakers) that they link their acceptance by others to "administering" unto them.

• Become professional "volunteers," routinely going beyond the call of duty to demonstrate their worth.

• Spend a lot of time trying to convince others what to

103

think, feel, and do (though here again, the underlying motive isn't so much to control others but to feel more secure in their relationship to them).

• Repeatedly do favors for, give gifts to, or anticipate the needs of others (though mostly to influence others' reactions to them—making their magnanimity a kind of bribe).

• Encourage others to let them be their caretaker or confidante—or otherwise become indispensable to them (in the hope of eliminating any chance of abandonment, which can be terrifying to them).

• Take on the role of problem-solver, decision-maker, support person, savior or rescuer (see immediately above).

• Use sex to optimize the chance of acceptance, confusing sex for real intimacy (which, given their past, is highly problematic [i.e., confusing] for them).

• Manipulate people and situations, by way of connecting or (artificially) bonding with them.

Note that in all these instances, the codependents' behavior—whether controlling, manipulative, supportive, super-responsible, sacrificial, or rescuing—is driven by the same never met childhood needs: to be fully, unconditionally accepted by their caretakers. And that includes being able to feel safe and protected, attended to, empathized with, respected, esteemed—in a word, nurtured. So in their seriously misguided adult quest for (unfortunately, conditional) relational acceptance, there's very little they won't do.

Moreover, as already suggested, despite the pretense of strength and a non-self-interested desire to serve others (rather than somehow inducing others to serve them), the underlying dependency of so much of their behavior should be obvious. For literally "giving themselves away" to others is experienced by them as necessary if they're to alleviate their self-doubts and self-perceived deficiencies. Their very sense of self (as inauthentic as it is) necessitates that they do all they can to receive others' approval. And they anticipate and cater to others' dependency needs mainly to shore up their shaky belief in their worthiness. Finally, not really trusting others (for they could never trust their parents—who inevitably became their models for "how to be" in relationships), their own carefully cultivated trustworthiness ironically sets them up to be taken advantage of (as, similarly, their needy caretakers exploited their normal childhood dependencies to take advantage of them).

9.2   Differences in a Codependency vs. an Interdependent Relationship

One of the best ways of really demonstrating the characteristics of a codependent relationship is by comparing it to a healthy, interdependent one. That's why we've put together a quick comparison between the two pointing out nine specific qualities and how they're manifested differently in each kind of relationship.

Freedom of Choice
Codependent relationships thrive off of possession and the need to keep the other partner guarded. Interdependent relationships celebrate individuality and give each party personal space for growth.

Defining Identities
Codependent relationships are threatened by individual differences and identities are completely intertwined. Interdependent relationships feature differences of personality or opinion that are respected and appreciated.
Attribution of Strength of Relationship
Codependent relationships are built on the strength of the other person or the control itself over the other person. Interdependent relationships attribute strength to two separate identities working together.

Volatility

Codependent relationships are highly volatile with intense ups and destructive Interdependent relationships are consistent and predictable with few spikes in intensity.

Support Systems

Codependent relationships shut out family, friends, and other social support staples in either one or both parties. Interdependent relationships have a broad support system with each member participating in activities and maintaining friendships outside of the relationship.

Influence on Mood

Codependent relationships feature members that are overwhelmingly affected by the emotions of the other (i.e. their bad day means you can only have a bad day). Interdependent relationships involve sympathy and empathy without taking on the pain or problem as one's own.

Evaluation & Criticism

Codependent relationships usually involve parties that are unwilling to confront the truth about deep problems in the relationship. Interdependent relationships are open to evaluation and change if it means the opportunity for growth.

Control

Codependent relationships are about the need to either control or are controlled by another. Interdependent relationships surrender power willingly only for the good of the relationship or the other person.

Honesty

Codependent relationships are built on lies, deceit, and manipulation. Interdependent relationships value honesty and   integrity.

CHAPTER 10

HOW TO RECLAIM YOUR LIFE FROM CODEPENDENCY

Here, are the steps to quit being codependent and reclaim your life.

1. Stop Forgetting to be Tender With Yourself First

When you are in a codependent relationship, you stay because you think you will not get anyone better. You might honestly believe you are lucky to have a partner who "puts up with you" or who is willing to be with you in the first place.

If you heard someone say that about your friend, though, you would think it was ridiculous. Nobody is doing anybody any favors by dating them, and romance is not a charity case. You are with somebody because you want to be with them — period, end of the story.

When you start valuing yourself and the contributions you give to your relationships, then you won't accept it when someone doesn't treat you with the respect you deserve. You'll be able to cut out problematic people from your life before they take root in it, and you will be able to recognize who makes you feel good, who makes you feel anxious, and why that anxiety doesn't actually mean you're in love.

Lifting yourself up and recognizing your own worth also

107

means you are able to provide yourself with care, tenderness, and love, and be patient with yourself and your feelings. That means when a new relationship does come into your life, you will know from the jump that you don't need them to make you happy. You already have yourself.

2.   Stop Thinking A Relationship Is A Key To Your Happiness

When you are in a codependent relationship, it might be hard to separate yourself from a partner in order to accomplish your goals. Your one and only goal might actually just be sustaining a relationship, even if it is with someone who is incapable of making you happy. Because you think that being with someone is the only thing that can bring you satisfaction, you start pouring all of your love and resources into a partnership that is imbalanced and not actually that good for you.

Leaning on a relationship as the main source of your security and self-esteem puts way too much pressure on your partner. It might even lead you to perceive yourself as needy or clingy, particularly if your partner claims you are needing too much maintenance in the relationship.

A relationship is just one small piece of the many things that can bring you a sense of joy and satisfaction. Start viewing your friends, your passions, and your ambitions as equally worthy of your time as dating or meeting someone. And when you do meet someone, evaluate them carefully. Is this someone you really want to be with? Or are you using them to fill an emotional void? Be honest and you'll find the answer.

3.   Get Some Clarity on What you Really Want iIn Life

It's a beautiful thing to build a life with a partner and strive for common goals, but you need to make sure that you don't lose sight of your own dreams too. If you do, it's something you may well come to regret.

Meditation and journaling are great ways to reflect on what your goals truly are and whether they're truly compatible with your partner's goals, and your goals as a couple. There's always going to be a certain amount of compromise involved, but you should both be compromising equally.

4. Use Boundaries to Detach With Love

Trying to control another person through fixing them, manipulating them, or enabling them is essentially living in the problem since it's not possible to control another person. To live in the solution, we need to detach from trying to change outcomes for another person and instead let them live their own life so that we can live our own life.

Enabling is when we do something for someone that they can do for themselves and need to do for themselves for their own growth. If we do it for them, we take away their power.

Enabling hinders the other person's development and even though it looks like helping, it's harming. So we must get out of the way. Detaching ourselves from their problem is actually the most loving thing we can do. The one and only person we can change is our own self.

5. Beware of Hooks

Hooks are common in codependent relationships and you may notice them pop up even more as you try to unhook yourself and the other person senses they are losing control over you. It's natural for people to dig their hooks in deeper if they feel threatened by a shift in the relationship dynamic. Hooks look like blaming and guilt-tripping and victimhood and martyrdom. Hooks usually involve one person taking zero responsibility for their part and somehow managing to make everything your fault. So the best thing to do here is to prepare yourself that it will happen.

6. Build Your Self-esteem

Codependence usually stems from a very low sense of self-esteem. It's almost as if you're saying with your actions "I'm not worth it to focus on so I'll focus on you instead." When we are stuck in a codependent cycle, we lose what little sense of self we had to begin with. The cure for codependence is then to build our self-esteem. This is no small feat when you have none. So we start where we are and we start small. We build esteem through caring for ourselves, and even if we don't feel worthy, we act like we are and eventually the belief catches on. We affirm ourselves in the mirror. We take care of our physical self through exercise, eating well, and maintaining personal hygiene. We get dressed and care for our appearance because it helps us to feel good about ourselves.

5 Life-Changing Habits That Build Self-Esteem

Our thoughts are powerful – for better or worse. Thoughts can set off chain reactions that build self-esteem or undermine it. Authority over our mind is the ultimate power. "Mind is everything. What you think you become,". Thoughts affect not only our mental health, relationships, and the ability to achieve our goals, but also our physical health – our digestion, circulation, respiration, immunity, and nervous system.

Next, are our actions. Change begins in the mind but is manifested and amplified by our actions. How we behave can change our thoughts and feelings. They change us.

Spend 15 minutes doing the following each day, and watch your whole life change:

1. Mindfulness

Mindfulness brings awareness to our thoughts. It's merely the ability to observe our thinking in a dispassionate, neutral way. Research has shown that mindfulness meditation has numerous benefits, including:

- Reduced rumination
- Reduced stress
- Increased working memory
- Increased ability to focus
- Increased empathy
- Increased self-esteem and self-compassion
- Reduced reactivity
- Increased cognitive flexibility

110

- Increased relationship satisfaction
- Increased speed of information processing
- Other benefits.

Mindfulness has been shown to enhance self-insight, morality, intuition and fear modulation, and other health and brain functioning benefits.

Shining the light of consciousness on our mental process differs from being caught up in thoughts and the stories we create and react to as if they were true. Observing thoughts tends to dissipate unhelpful, repetitive ones and helps free us from self-judgment and the need to control. Mindfulness also brings us into the present moment, in contrast to the focusing on achieving or fixing things or being lost in obsessive thoughts about other people, the past, or future. It increases our ability to question, challenge, replace, or stop our thoughts and actions. In this way, we're better able to make constructive changes and avoid repeating past mistakes.

Mindfulness also changes how we perceive reality so that events don't automatically affect us and our self-concept. We develop the ability to experience reality in a non-evaluative manner and less reactive way. Because our self-worth is less dependent on external reality, we're able to embrace our inner-self rather than relying on others for validation. There is evidence that high levels of mindfulness correlate with higher levels of self-esteem and more secure self-worth.

2. Our thoughts are powerful – for better or worse. Thoughts can set off chain reactions that build self-esteem or undermine it. Authority over our mind is the ultimate power. "Mind is everything. What you think you become," said Buddha. Thoughts affect not only our mental health, relationships, and the ability to achieve our goals, but also our physical health – our digestion, circulation, respiration, immunity, and nervous system.

Next, are our actions. Change begins in the mind but is manifested and amplified by our actions. How we behave can change our thoughts and feelings. They change us. Spend 15 minutes doing the following each day, and watch your whole life change:

start replacing the negative with positive, self-affirming statements. Beware, however, that if you tell yourself things you don't believe, your efforts can backfire. Your unconscious is very literal and doesn't distinguish between what you tell yourself and what others say to you.

3. Make a Gratitude List

Cultivating "An attitude of gratitude" has numerous health and psychological benefits. Among them, studies show that it will:

- Increased quality sleep
- Increased time exercising
- Increased vitality and energy
- Increased physical and psychological health
- Increased empathy
- Increased self-esteem
- Increase productivity and decision-making ability
- Increased resiliency in overcoming trauma
- Reduced depression (by a whopping 35%)

It can be hard to feel grateful when you don't, especially when you have depression, anxiety, trauma, or physical pain. An easy way to begin is to keep a daily journal and write 3-10 things you're grateful for. In doing this daily, your mind will start looking for things each day to add to your list. In this way, your outlook on life begins to change. You'll have even greater benefits if you do this with a friend, sponsor, or your partner and read your list aloud. Here are more tips on developing gratitude.

4. Make a Plan

Not only has research shown that goal setting increases both motivation and performance, it also enhances positive feelings and our sense of well-being, self-efficacy, success, and job satisfaction. Each day writes daily objectives. For me, it works better to do this the night before. If you have a lot on your mind that interferes with falling asleep, making a to-do list can get them off your mind. It's important not to abandon yourself. When you don't feel like doing something, like paying bills or exercising, do it anyway. Larger goals require more thought and planning, but research shows that the more difficult the goal, the greater the pay-off. This makes sense since the greater achievement would build more self-confidence and self-esteem. When you have a bigger goal, break it down into small, daily, actionable steps.

5. Do Esteemable Acts

Actions count a lot. Doing things in line with your values that raises your self-esteem and elevates your mood. Conversely, doing things that make you feel ashamed or guilty undermines self-worth. Aside from living in accordance with our values, such as not lying or stealing, making an effort to do things that build self-esteem pays off.

Plan to do one each day. Examples are:

• Writing a thank you note
• Sending birthday cards
• Calling a sick friend
• Cleaning out a closet
• Staying on top of filing, bill-paying, etc. (not procrastinating)
• Volunteering to help someone or a group
• Setting a boundary
• Speaking up about your wants and needs
• Showing appreciation to others
• Apologizing when you're wrong
• Making a special meal
• Self-care, including keeping medical appointments

All this may sound like too much and too time-consuming, but mediating a mere 10 minutes a day develops a healthy habit. It can take less than 5 minutes to write goals for the day, a grateful list, and negative and positive self-talk. At the end of the day, you can write three things you did well, and feel grateful and proud. Go to sleep with a smile, knowing that you improved yourself and your life.

Conclusion

Codependency has grown in meaning to keep up with the challenges of a changing society and it can be a misunderstood, overused and also wrongly used term. While in some ways we have all shown codependent behaviors, to suffer from full codependency is different and is a real emotional and sometimes lifelong struggle that often requires therapy to overcome. It's important that we don't allow the flippancy with which people now use the word codependency to diminish the real pain and suffering those who are truly codependent suffer.

Codependency is above all a mistaken seeking for love by those who have only ever been shown the control when growing up and have therefore mistaken control for love. And can any of us honestly judge anyone on wanting to be cared for and loved?

From what mentioned, it can be concluded that not all addicts' spouses experienced codependency. Women under stress of living with addicts were high in neuroticism and low in openness and agreeableness, probably because they perceive the situation more stressful and use less effective coping strategies; then, they will be vulnerable against the stressors and experience codependency, as the consequence of these circumstances.

Codependency is not only mentally unhealthy; it can even be dangerous. The person who is dependent on you may sink deeper into their addictions or mental illness. This can sometimes lead to aggressive and hostile behaviors toward themselves and loved ones, including you.